CLARITY FOR YOUR CREATIVE CAREER:
TIPS, ADVICE AND INSPIRATION FROM SUCCESSFUL ARTISTS TO QUIT THE JOB YOU HATE & CREATE A LIFE YOU LOVE

CLARITY

FOR YOUR
CREATIVE CAREER:

Tips, advice and inspiration from successful artists to quit the job you hate & create a life you love

LAURA MEOLI-FERRIGON

Convey Media, Inc.
New York

LoudaVision and design are trademarks of Laura Meoli-Ferrigon, the author of this work. Podcast profile photos courtesy of their respective photographers and producers. Convey Media is a registered trademark of Convey Media, Inc.

ISBN 978-0-9992375-2-6 paperback
ISBN 978-0-9992375-3-3 ebook

Designed by Sara B. Caldwell.

Text set in Adobe Caslon Pro, Permanent Marker, and Myriad Pro.
Published by Convey Media, Inc., New Rochelle, NY.

Contents

DEDICATION + THANKS

This book is dedicated to everyone who has participated in the LoudaVision Podcast for creative people. Thanks to the listeners, supporters and my expert guests. Also thanks to the participants of my freelance survey who shared details about their journey. Another big thank you to Dr. Alma who I initially interviewed for a documentary on the relationship between work and mindfulness. At the time, I never imagined I would be able to use her inspiring words to help me accomplish one of my lifetime goals.

Special thanks to the pre-sale contributors for my Indiegogo campaign, especially Christopher Coulter, Nancy Samuel, Donna Actie, Oscar Silva and Nina Stivala.

Each of my podcast guests have inspired me or helped me through an important question in my life. The podcast interviews were so well timed, and at times I felt that I was just using it to reach out to people for advice on whatever I was going through at the time: spiritually, emotionally and career-wise. I want to thank each of you individually, but also as a group, I want to express my gratitude for sharing your honest stories and life-lessons in a way that has improved my life. Now with this book, I know that our message will help others as well.

Thank you, Michelle for believing in me when I didn't believe in my own ability to host alone.

Anahita and Arta, thank you for challenging me to think about creativity and art on a deeper level, and connecting spirituality into the mix.

Barbara and Elaine, you are such strong and inspirational women who have pushed me to dream beyond the limits of my imagination and expectations for life.

Thank you, Gabrielle for bringing my AD notes and shot breakdowns to Brooklyn College when you were sick with the flu. Also for being a great filmmaker who always finds a way to get sh*t done.

Angela and Julia, thank you for showing me that it's okay to be silly and use my voice to express my authentic qualities. You helped me connect with my students in a way I never thought possible.

John, your book is fantastic. The way you connected spiritual principles to crowdfunding helped me finally feel comfortable inviting people to experience my work.

Alex Bondarev, thank you for helping me appreciate the deeper meaning behind my creative work, and the immense value of helping others.

Squeaky Moore and Teraj: What can't you do? Seriously I am so in awe your multiple areas of success and use that as a principle to live my life. Never settle for just one thing- go for it all.

Valentin, thank you for shooting 'CTV' and putting up with me. Our conversation about creativity and money will be forever cherished, and I am in awe of your courage and talent.

Suzanne, thank you for reminding me that I already know the answers deep down inside, but often forget. Your techniques and words of wisdom are amazing, and the Rock/Star Life Planner helped me make one of the most important decisions in my life.

Lina, thank you for pushing me to think carefully about my next move and inspiring me to take a leap of faith.

Janis, you reminded me of the importance that our health has on our life choices. Thank you for showing me that it is possible to still be successful without fighting my body.

Alex Wood and Mayra Ramales, you are both proof that we don't have to wait around for someone to create our platform for us. Just roll up our sleeves and create it for ourselves, so we can share our gifts with the world.

Jacob zzzBubs Bacaner, from college to successful entrepreneur, to whatever is next, your enthusiasm is contagious and pushes me to learn new things each day.

Brett Solomano's 28 Day Fear Challenge (Momentum Mastery) gave me the kick in the butt needed to set realistic goals, and finally write my book. Thanks, mate. (PS: You have an accent.)

Temica Gross, thank you sis. Your coaching and support has been instrumental in helping me realize my unique contributions as an entrepreneur and content creator.

Finally, last but not least, Magdalena. Thank you for proofreading, supporting... everything. You inspire me to let go of the assumptions I have about myself and push into a new creative stratosphere.

I couldn't have written this book without support and encouragement from Nina, Magdalena, Alvin and my work-buddy Hamburglar. Special thanks to my parents Anthony & Pamela Meoli for always encouraging and accepting my creativity, and for letting me go to film school when I had no exact plan of what that was going to become.

This book was edited by Phillip Ferrigon & Magdalena Polec. Interviews produced by LoudaVision Productions. Cover design and publishing by Convey Media, Inc.

Thank you to Winston Mitchell, Amanda Perez, Temica Gross and all the wonderful mentors I've had on this journey so far. To all the filmmakers, TV pros, podcasters and friends I've worked with in the past 10 years, thank you for pushing me to work harder and use criticism to grow.

Heartfelt gratitude to my acupuncturist Anabelle who helps me find natural ways to feel healthy. Also, Carmen and Carl for their spiritual guidance. I couldn't accomplish anything without a healthy mind and body.

Finally, massive thanks to my immensely encouraging husband Phillip. He helps with production and sharing my work on social media, among the million other ways he inspires me each day. Thank you for everything, my love.

INTRODUCTION

Are you unhappy with your career? If you hate your day job, you might imagine getting up from your desk and busting out those doors midday in a dramatic fashion. With shades on, wearing some sort of flowy cape or scarf, you leave all the stresses of the office behind you and strut out the door in slow motion.

What makes this a fantasy and not reality, is the question of what you might do after you walk out those doors. How will you make money to survive?

If you've thought about starting your own business, it can be hard to juggle the responsibilities of a startup along with your day job which pays the bills. We would all love more time in our day, away from our 9-to-5 to work on the creative projects that personally satisfy us. This leads us to the subject for which I have spent years researching:

How can we make money doing what we love?

There is an alternative to being a starving, struggling artist. This book consolidates years of research from my interviews with successful artists, visionaries and innovators into an easy guide to create the career you love. Being an artist is no longer a disadvantage in today's job market. I will present perspectives on creative entrepreneurship that can help you identify and achieve personal success. This book is for anyone who feels too creative for a traditional 9 to 5. If you are considering a shift in careers and are wondering about the reality of freelancing, this book shares the good and bad of both sides without ignoring the fact that money makes the world go round. Rather than quitting your job on a whim, this book will help you make informed decisions about your next move.

I am an Emmy award winning multimedia content creator and educator with 10 years in the film and television industry. Back when I was stuck working an unfulfilling 9-to-5, I started the LoudaVision Podcast for creative people. This podcast was a way for me to meet and interview new and interesting people. It was MY project for which I had complete creative control, and I didn't need endless layers of corporate approval (the way I did at my day job). The people I interviewed on the LoudaVision Podcast range from successful entrepreneurs and freelancers to creatives with passion projects they are working on outside of their full time day job to pay the bills. In this book you will find the best advice from these experts, taken directly from my interviews with them on the LoudaVision Podcast. I will also share my personal story, including how I quit my day job in 2017 to become a freelancer, and whether or not it was worth it.

This is not a self-help book that claims to have a step by step solution for you to quit your day job. This is a solutions guide for responsible adults who have bills to pay, and want to make an informed decision about their career. I do not claim to have created the exercises in this book. However, I have modified and combined a number of techniques, and ideally you will continue to modify my suggestions to work best for you. The tips in this solutions guide are customizable to fit your unique personality, so you can define and achieve your own success.

There are tons of books and tutorials out there promising you financial independence without putting in the work needed to build your business or achieve success. I know this because I've read these books and watched those tutorials. They might work for some people, but as an artist there is no cookie cutter guide that works for all of us. A success story for one might be a disaster for another. My aim in writing this book is to not insult your intelligence by promising a specific solution for everyone who reads it. This book will give you courage to make informed decisions about your unique career by offering nontraditional solutions from proven experts. I will give you both sides of the freelance versus full time debate. I'll break down the reality of working for yourself, positives and negatives. I will then offer solutions that will help you find clarity so you can achieve creative expression and fulfillment in your work, while making money so you can live your best life.

Don't let years of your life pass you by at a job that lets your potential go to waste. Use your passion to become an expert in your chosen field. Use your skills to make the money you deserve. Use your creativity to design the lifestyle you want.

The tips and tricks in this book are proven solutions to release you from the grips of fear. These real-life stories are designed to offer you creative alternatives to the life choices that you think you have to select from. Each chapter will explore different options, and then offer you an opportunity to decide if this is right for you, based on your own personal experience. Whether you want to quit your day job, or if you already have and wish you hadn't, all you have to do is keep reading if you want to create a life of abundance.

Meet the Experts

Let's take a moment to meet some of the people you will be hearing from in this book. The following are guests from the LoudaVision podcast for creative people. I created this podcast to break the stereotype of the starving and struggling artist by sharing ways to make money without sacrificing happiness. Experts discuss what it takes to succeed in the arts, and methods for bringing your creative vision to life. Although I did not expect to be re-purposing this content, it was only natural that I would use these interviews to inspire me to make a huge lifestyle shift, and to write this book that will hopefully inspire and inform you.

Podcast Guests:

Michelle Engberg is a professional photographer and pixel artist who revels in creating world-class results for local businesses as well as some of the world's most distinct global brands. Michelle's experience is in fashion, editorial, catalog, beauty, portrait and fine art photography. She can make great photos into beautiful editorial layouts and print-perfect press files by combining her expert skill-set with her amazing creativity and state-of-the-art technology. Michelle Engberg Provides services in Phoenix, AZ, Las Vegas, NV, Los Angeles, CA and New York, NY. www.michelleengberg.com

Anahita Moghaddam is the founder of Neural Beings, a coach and speaker who's rigorous and experiential methodology is rooted in the Eastern contemplative traditions, and continuously refined under the mentorship of leading scientists and academics in the

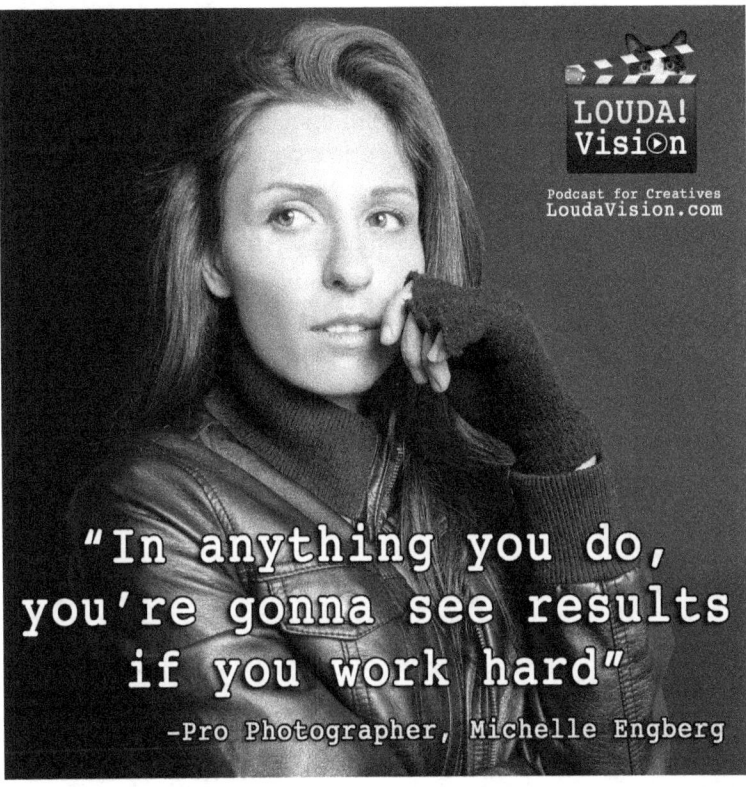

"In anything you do, you're gonna see results if you work hard"
-Pro Photographer, Michelle Engberg

fields of psychology, philosophy, neuroscience and biology.

Anahita was born in Tehran, raised in Hamburg and attended university in London. She has worked in media and journalism for European news agencies, and produced macro-economic country reports for Forbes, the Washington Post and The Times. She has lived and worked in Croatia, Botswana, Indonesia and the Arab Emirates, interviewing senior political and business leaders, while gaining insight into the mindsets of a wide array of individuals.

Anahita's clients include executives, entrepreneurs, UN staff, diplomats, as well as leaders in hospitality, design, technology and social innovation. She has facilitated workshops on the Neuroscience of Mindfulness at the 2014 Feast Conference for Social Good, featured on Entrepreneur.com, and led a Masterclass at the 2015

Social Media Week NY, featured on HuffPost Live. Anahita has led workshops at The Harvard Business School Club NY, Soho House NY, The 88, Hackster, The Lowell Hotel, Civic Hall and more.

Anahita holds a BA in Marketing and Advertising, from the London College of Communication and an MA in Social Anthropology, from the School of Oriental and African Studies London. She is further training in Contemplative Psychotherapy at the Nalanda Institute for Contemplative Science in New York, under the guidance of Dr. Miles Neale and Dr. Joe Loizzo.

Anahita has been a student of meditation, yoga, philosophy and epistemology within the Indo-Tibetan tradition for over a decade. She is also a dancer, trained in modern, Latin, African and Persian Sufi whirling, and practices Muay Thai. www.neuralbeings.com

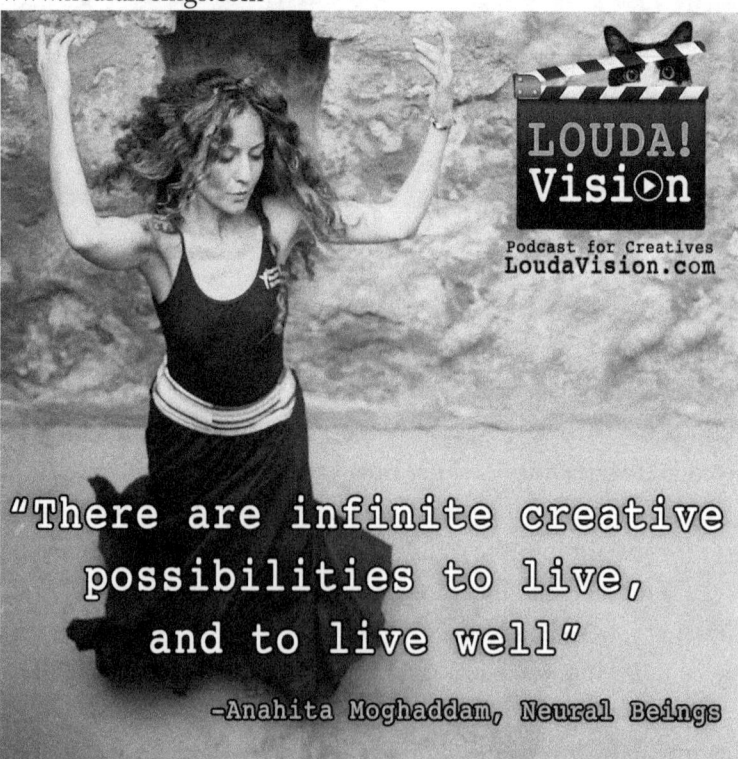

LOUDA! Vision
Podcast for Creatives
LoudaVision.com

"There are infinite creative possibilities to live, and to live well"

—Anahita Moghaddam, Neural Beings

Elaine Del Valle was born & raised in Brownsville, Brooklyn (New York). She began her entertainment career as an actress, and found early success in the commercial and voice over markets. While studying acting under the legendary Wynn Handman at Carnegie Hall, Elaine developed what became her multiple award winning, autobiographical one-woman stage play, Brownsville Bred.

Brownsville Bred chronicled Elaine's true New York Puerto Rican coming-of-age story— Set in the tough projects of Brownsville Brooklyn, NY, in the 1980's, Elaine's story brought resilience, love and laughter to a world filled with crime, heroine-addiction, AIDS, and welfare.—Her Off Broadway debut brought critical acclaim. The New York Times called it "From Girlhood Trials to Onstage Triumph." (*Photo Credit: Taryn Kosviner*)

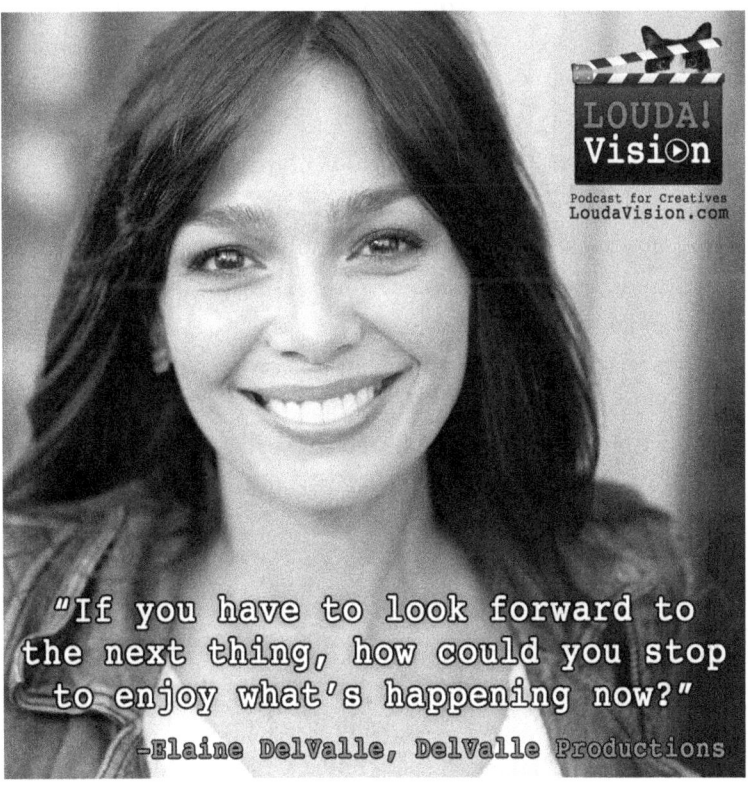

LOUDA!
Visi◉n
Podcast for Creatives
LoudaVision.com

"If you have to look forward to the next thing, how could you stop to enjoy what's happening now?"
-Elaine DelValle, DelValle Productions

With a deep understanding of her truthful writing's impact, Elaine founded Del Valle Productions, Inc. —a full service, bilingual film production and casting company with a mission: to infuse entertainment with original programming using diverse talent in front of and behind the camera. Elaine was named "Trendsetter" at New York's Multicultural Media Forum and "Madrina/Godmother" by Prime Latino Media. Her company has gone on to produce multiple films, and has a casting division (Del Valle Casting) that has cast actors for major market commercials, in television & digital series, theater and in feature films.

An accomplished producer, Elaine was the first to license an interstitial series (her co-production of Gran'pa Knows Best) to the HBO Latino Network. She received a 2016 Telly award for her co-production of PBS/World Channel series, The Smallest Step. Elaine co-created, co-wrote, produced and directed the comedy web series, Reasons Y I'm Single (now on Amazon Prime). Elaine has also directed commercials (in English and Spanish) and in 2017 she penned Final Decision, which marked Elaine's directorial debut in a short film. While on the 2017 festival circuit, Final Decision played at over a dozen festivals, winning Del Valle two "Best Actor" awards, a "Best Narrative Director in a Short Film" award and a "Best Original Film Score" award. Del Valle's many film productions continue to win awards across festivals including the short hybrid animation documentary, Victor & Isolina— which has won numerous awards, screened at over 50 festivals (including the 2017 Sundance Film Festival), IFP Film Center, and at The MoMA. Elaine recently licensed Victor & Isolina to HBO where it will premiere in 2018.

Elaine is represented as an actress by Headline Talent Agency. She continues to act in film and television, and in 2018 will direct and produce her short film series based on her play, Brownsville Bred. Elaine Del Valle was named "Trendsetter" at the MultiCultural Media Forum and a CNN "Woman of Note."

In 2015, she received the "Madrina" Award for her contribution to Latino Entertainment. She has been recognized by CNN en Español, The Hispanic Organization for Latin Actors, Fox News, NBC News, the New York Times, The Daily News, Red Shoe Movement, Latin Trends, and American Latino TV, amongst others. www.delvallecasting.com

Jacob Bacaner is an entrepreneur, fitness model and coach who went from Morgan Stanley to Elite Models Miami. Jacob's free online course will teach you how to start your own landscaping and cleaning business on Nextdoor.com.
www.youtube.com/user/jacobbacaner
www.HowtoStartaLandscapingBusinessonNextDoorApp.com

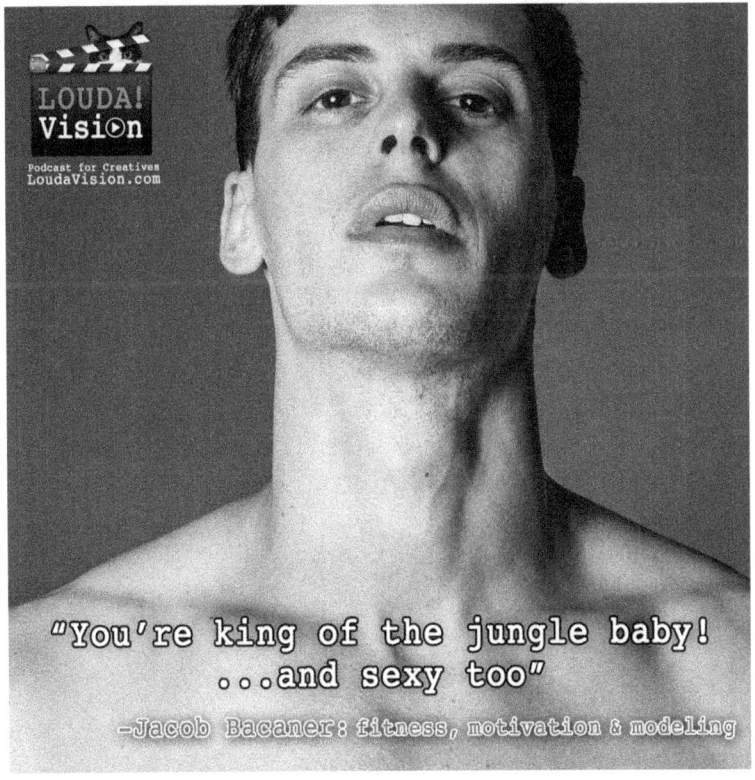

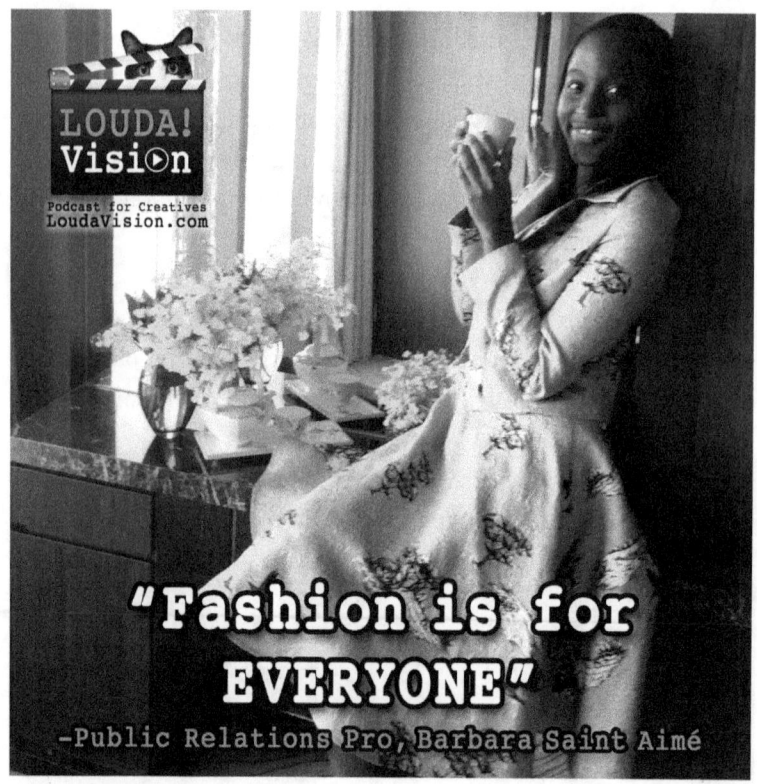

"Fashion is for EVERYONE"

-Public Relations Pro, Barbara Saint Aimé

Barbara Saint Aime was born in Haiti and moved to New York at the age of four. In 2008 she earned her bachelor's degree in mass communications from St. Francis College. While attending college she also interned at NBC Universal Pictures in the publicity department. Upon graduating she was hired at BWR public relations, where she worked for six years. At BWR, Barbara honed her skills as a PR professional, working closely with the President of the company. Barbara founded Aime Agency in 2014. She is excited to work on emerging talent and develop them into household names. www.aimeagency.com

Angela Star is a stand-up comedian, host and motivational speaker born and raised in the mean streets of Brooklyn, NY. Her passion for comedy began at a young age, when using jokes helped her overcome life's everyday struggles and embarrassing moments growing up less fortunate than everyone around her (AKA poor).

Star continues to entertain and shock audiences across the city performing at notable comedy clubs such as Caroline's on Broadway, Gotham Comedy Club, Broadway Comedy Club and New York Comedy Club. She also travels hosting and performing throughout the United States and internationally in the Caribbean, Canada and China. Star is known for her versatility, performing for mature audiences in addition to delivering clean material at various churches, schools and government organizations. She is a

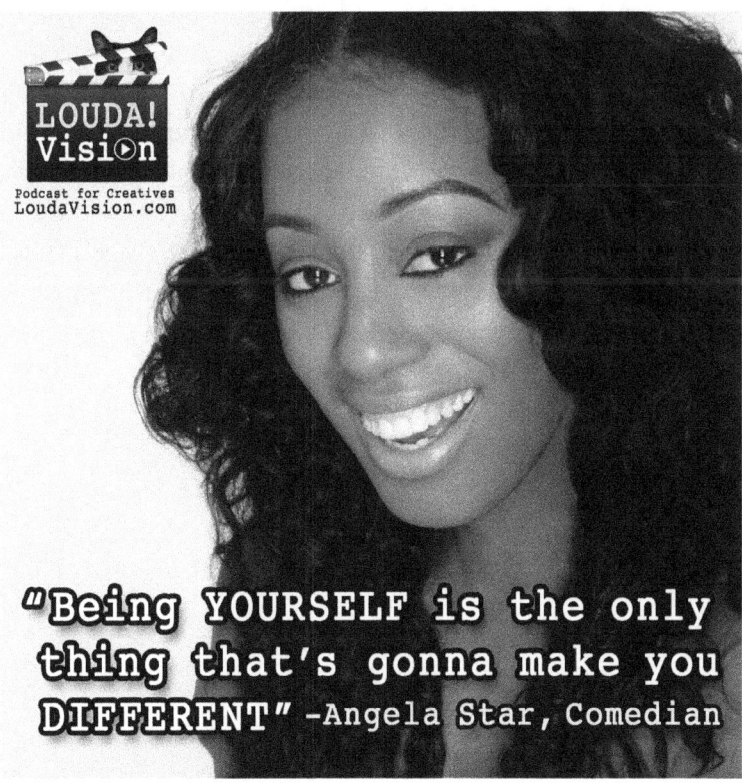

LOUDA!
Visi⦿n
Podcast for Creatives
LoudaVision.com

"Being YOURSELF is the only thing that's gonna make you DIFFERENT" -Angela Star, Comedian

supporter for the deaf and hard of hearing, using ASL (American Sign Language) to promote deaf culture awareness at various colleges, special events and ASL slams.

Star is an advocate for the "Office of Minority Health and Health Disparities Prevention." She uses humor as a powerful tool to spread health related messages, increase awareness and educate underserved populations affected by health disparities. Her memorable comedic spin on these health issues has helped capture the attention of target audiences, making them more receptive to the important health messages at hand.

Star is also the founder of "Stars of Comedy" a youth after school program that helps kids develop their comedic talents, build and strengthen performance techniques, and learn about the industry. She currently teaches 3rd, 5th and 8th grade in various schools throughout Brooklyn, NY.

In addition to her love for comedy, Star also enjoys reading comics, sneakers, UFC, sleeping on the train and has been told that she's easy on the eyes by men, women and transvestites. She is a natural born performer with a strong drive and passion for comedy. Filled with incredible stage presence, Angela Star's comedic style is random yet relatable with a hint of surprise. www.astarsmentality.com

Alex Wood is co-founder of Honelife.com and the Variety Seeker Tribe, along with his sister Jessica. They formed this group for people who are fed up with "searching for their passion," and who want something more than a conventional existence, to connect with others who share the same desire to live extraordinary lives. www.Honelife.com

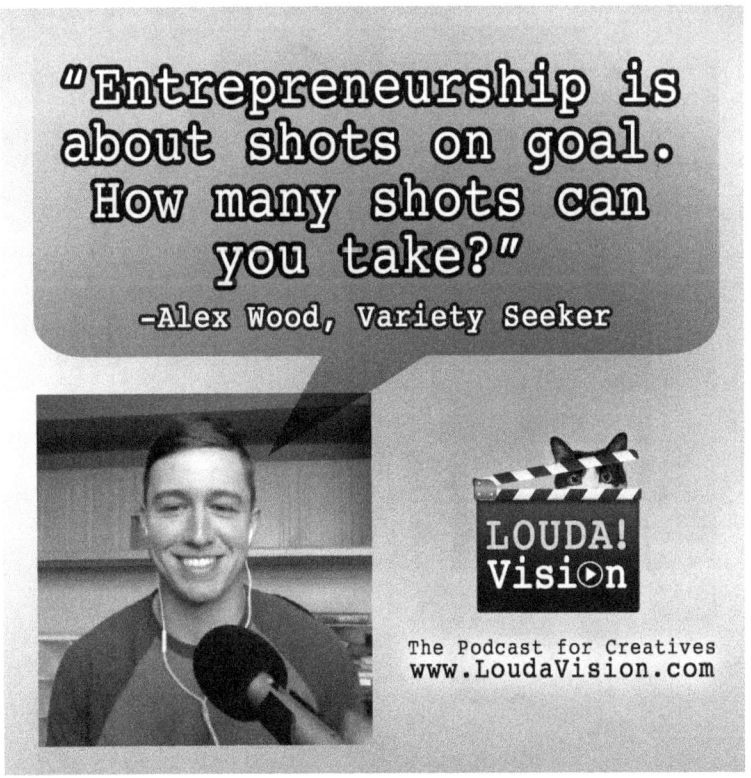

"Entrepreneurship is about shots on goal. How many shots can you take?"

-Alex Wood, Variety Seeker

LOUDA! Vision

The Podcast for Creatives
www.LoudaVision.com

Gabrielle Aliké Hawkins graduated from Brooklyn College with a B.A. in Film Production. She studied at The Met Film School in London where she studied producing and received a Certificate of Completion. Gabrielle has worked on short films, features and music videos. She started as a production assistant working in music videos with artists such as Beyonce, The Roots, and John Legend. She worked with top music video directors Gil Green and Dayo Harewood. Her film work includes working on the critically acclaimed Chris Rock film "Top Five." She also worked on "Will of Fortune" directed by Chloe Bellande which premiered at the Cannes Film Festival. At the age of 27, she worked as an assistant director on the award-winning film "Alto" directed by Mikki Del Monico. *(Photo Credit: Brandon Haynes)*

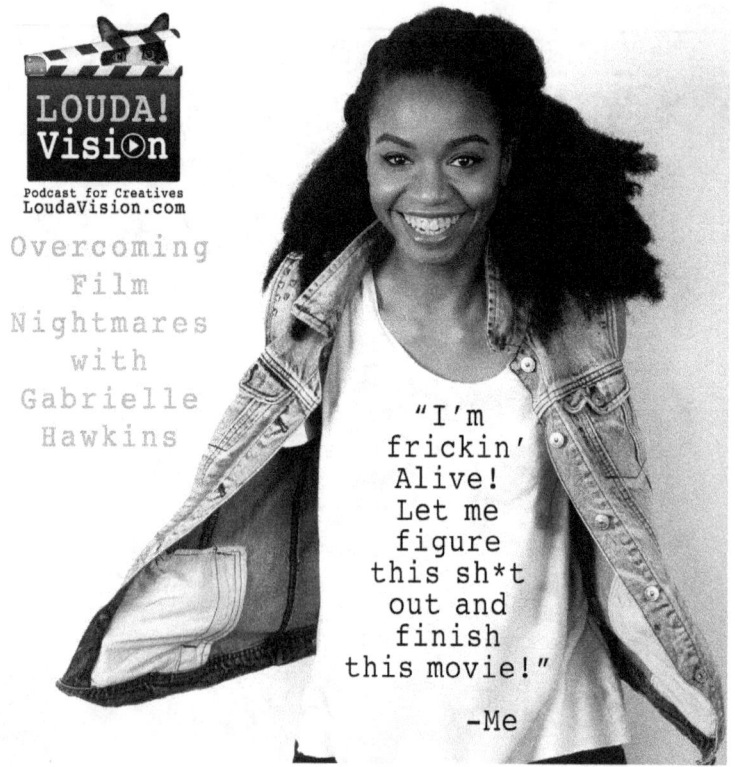

LOUDA!
Visi⏵n

Podcast for Creatives
LoudaVision.com

Overcoming
Film
Nightmares
with
Gabrielle
Hawkins

"I'm
frickin'
Alive!
Let me
figure
this sh*t
out and
finish
this movie!"

-Me

Gabrielle is also a photographer and in 2012 had a 4-day exhibition of her 7-picture series called "States of Minds." The series was also part of the Brooklyn Waterfront Artists Coalition (BWAC) in Redhook, Brooklyn.

Her short film "Criminals" is now an official selection in multiple festivals, and winner of the 2017 NYC Indie Film Award. www.gabriellealikehawkins.com

Lina Lansky found her passion for media and film while working as a volunteer host for Transit Transit News Magazine's TV show at the Metropolitan Transportation Authority. While pursuing a Masters Degree in Business Administration, Lina questioned whether or not to drop the program and go for a film degree. She decided to push through and learn as much as possible about the film industry on the side. After some time she started her own LLC, and tried to jump start a video production company having no prior experience running a business. She soon realized that the endeavor was far harder than she imagined. After a few event gigs, a music video and a documentary Lina and her business partner went separate ways.

In the winter of 2016, Lina made the decision to quit her full time 9-to-5 job, and pursue freelance in the film industry. She got her first break when a Director she had worked with in the past asked her to be an Assistant Director for her feature film. Since then Lina has been a 1st Assistant Director for two feature films,

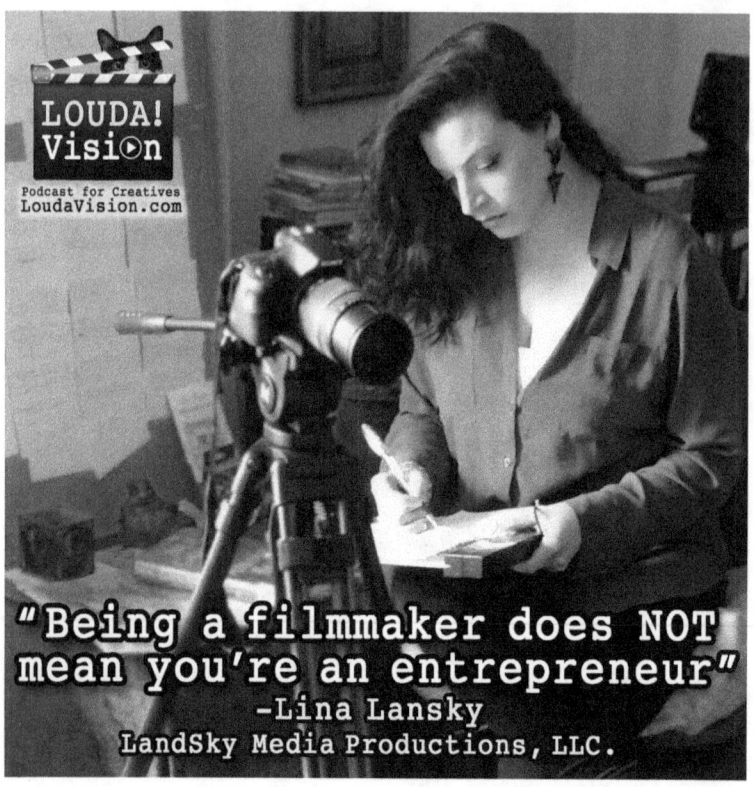

"Being a filmmaker does NOT mean you're an entrepreneur"
-Lina Lansky
LandSky Media Productions, LLC.

three music videos, a short, and has been a 2nd Assistant Director for a SAG feature. Lina hopes that 2018 will bring more Assistant Directing, and Producer opportunities her way.

Janis Vogel is a professional editor born in Germany and raised on Martha's Vineyard. Her work includes television series, narrative films, music videos and promotional pieces. She most recently worked on Spike Lee's remake of She's Gotta Have It, for Netflix as one of two assistant editors on the series. After studying at Wellesley College, she went on to receive her M.F.A.

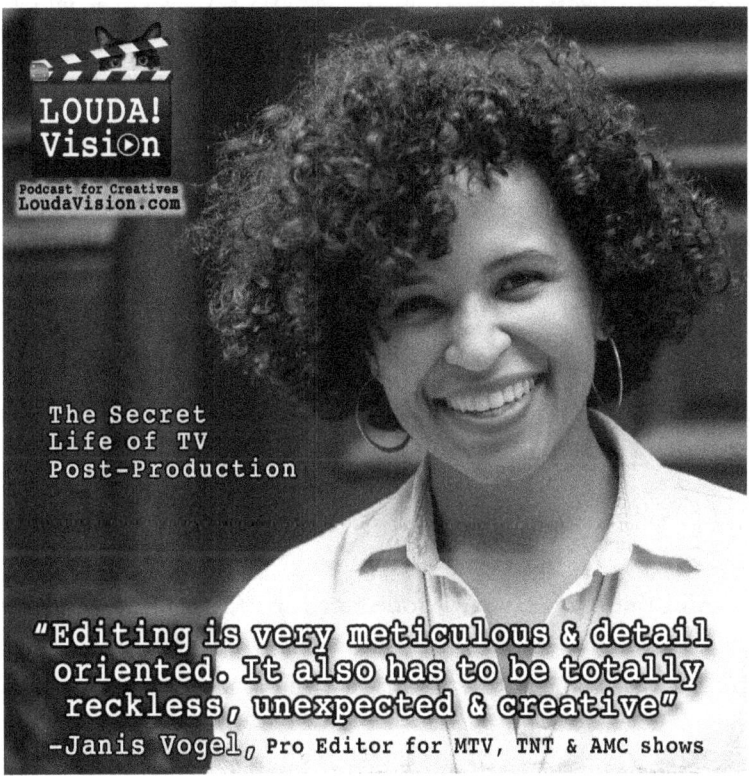

LOUDA!
Visi⊙n

Podcast for Creatives
LoudaVision.com

The Secret
Life of TV
Post-Production

"Editing is very meticulous & detail oriented. It also has to be totally reckless, unexpected & creative"
-Janis Vogel, Pro Editor for MTV, TNT & AMC shows

in film from the City College of New York. Her thesis film Drop, which she wrote, directed, and edited, won her the Independent Film Project and New York Mayor's Office of Film's NextGen Award. She has produced, shot and edited documentary series' for MTV, DISCOVERY, TLC, and OWN and music videos for artists including TEEN, Dual Split, and Justin

Vivien-Bond. She has shot and edited projects for director Silas Howard, such as the short documentary, Sticks & Stones: Bambi Lake, which premiered at Outfest. *(Photo Credit: Katie Hinsen)* She has edited a number of short films, directed by Julia Thompson, including Bright In Here which premiered at the Queens Film Festival. Janis is also the co-founder of the non-profit organization The Blue Collar Post Collective, which advocates for a more accessible and inclusive film industry. www.Janisvogel.com

Alex Bondarev is a New York-based artist, and a Russian-born refugee who has grown up in the Bronx and has found solace in introspective songwriting. His solo indie music project is Conversing with Oceans.

Since its inception in 2015, CWO has garnered the attention of Randy Jackson at SXSW, collaborated with the Grammy-nominated John Forte, has been featured on NPR, and has maintained an active partnership with the SF-based nonprofit Elfenworks, working closely together to inspire hope and give back to their community. The latest Trilogy EP with producer-engineer Tim O'Sullivan (Childish Gambino, Karen O) is available everywhere now via The Orchard.

Conversing with Oceans has been featured on NPR, *(Photo Credit: Rosemarie Elizabeth Photography)* Apple Music & iTunes homepages, trended on Hype Machine, headlined Studio at Webster Hall, released two EPs (Indie Films & Trilogy), and have fought to Stand Against Hate in our community.

Aiming for a full-length album in 2018 and to keep giving back. Since our podcast, Alex and his wife welcomed a baby girl who has become his world. www.conversingwithoceans.com

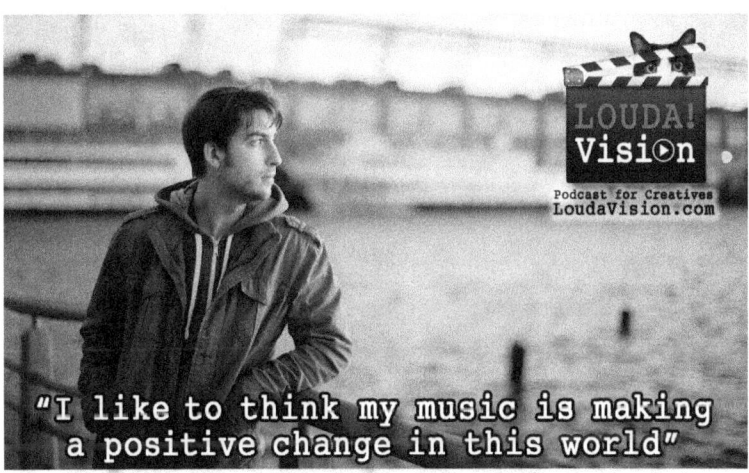

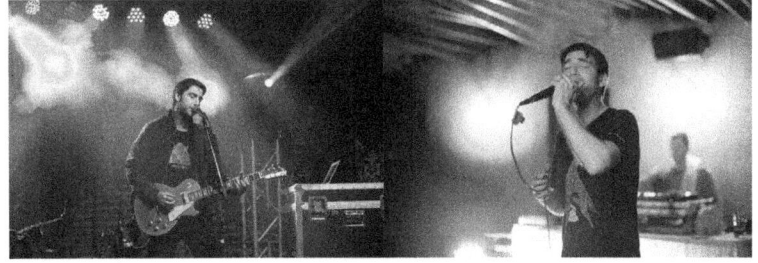

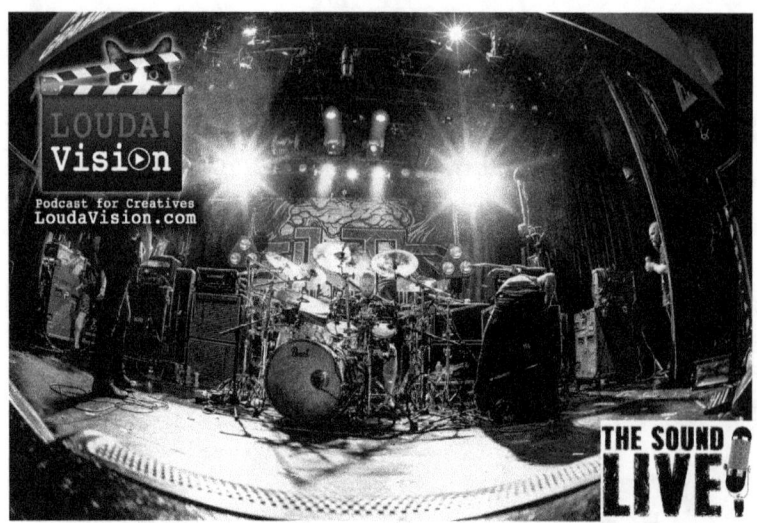

"Don't feel like you have to wait for
someone to open that door for you.
You can definitely create it yourself"
    -Mayra Ramales, Founder of TheSoundLive.com

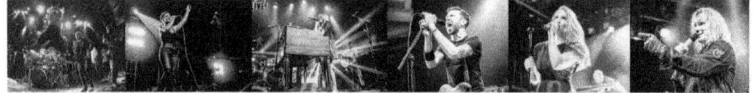

Mayra Ramales is a music and sports enthusiast currently the manager of TheSoundLive.com and contributor to MMA sports website TodaysKnockout.com and LowKickMMA.com. Her passion for writing and photography has led her to create a platform for other fellow writers and photographers to expand their portfolio as contributors to The Sound Live. Artists photographed include Slipknot, Sarah McLachlan, and Mumford & Sons. Her love for music transcends genres and go from heavy metal all the way to soul and country. She hopes to share her love for the arts in order to help others improve their skills and enjoy live music at the same time. www.theSoundLive.com

Arta Cakaj is a mother, a Licensed Creative Arts Therapist, and an artist. She provides Art therapy and Psychotherapy to children, adolescents, and adults in her private practice Wholehearted Creative Arts Therapy in Mamaroneck, Westchester. Art therapy integrates artistic expression into the healing process. It can be emotionally restorative and can serve as an outlet for expressing feelings. Art reaches deep places in our unconscious where words are unreachable. Arta's approach is to see everyone as a whole human being: Mind, Body and Spirit. Every client is unique therefore her therapy is tailored and individualized based on individual needs. She is passionate about her work and loves what she does. www.wholeheartedarttherapy.com

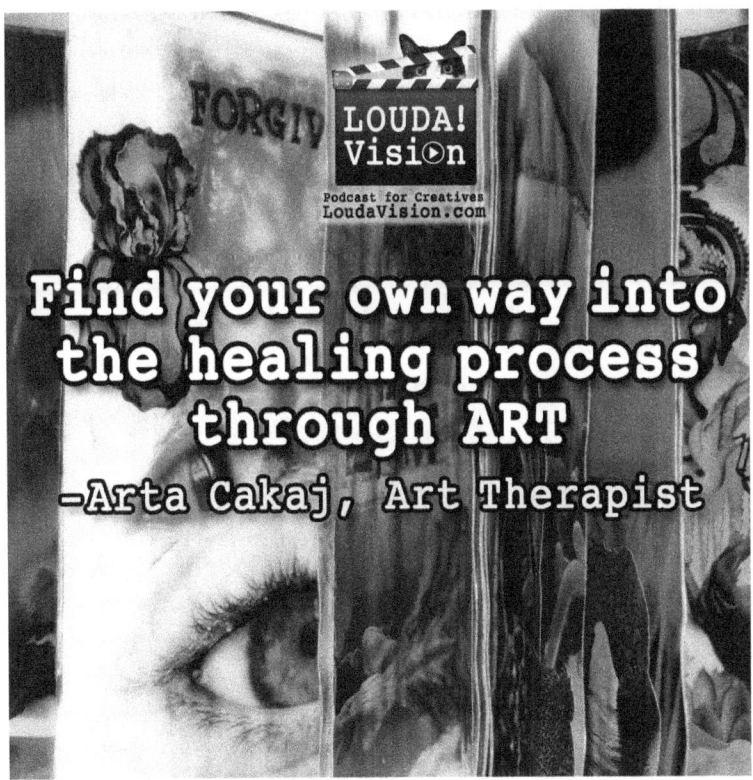

Suzanne Paulinski started out in the music industry as an intern for Atlantic Records and college rep for WEA. After graduating with a B.S. in Music Industry from Drexel University, she managed the national street team & Midwest retail for Astralwerks (EMI) before going on to work as a paralegal and complete her Masters in Psychology at Queens College (CUNY). Now, with The Rock/Star Advocate, she is a mindset coach for creatives, helping them reach their goals by learning to see themselves as entrepreneurs while maintaining a healthy work/life balance. She published her first book, The Rock/Star Life Planner, now in its third edition on Amazon. Her teachings can also be found in her many guest posts for Huffington Post, Sonicbids, ReverbNation, CD Baby, Tunecore, and Soundfly.

Since our podcast, Suz hosted her first live music summit in Rehoboth Beach, DE - The Music-Preneur Mindset Summit. You can read about it in HuffPo. She also published the latest edition of the rock/star life planner on Amazon.

(*Photo Credit: Kon Boogie*)

www.therockstaradvocate.com

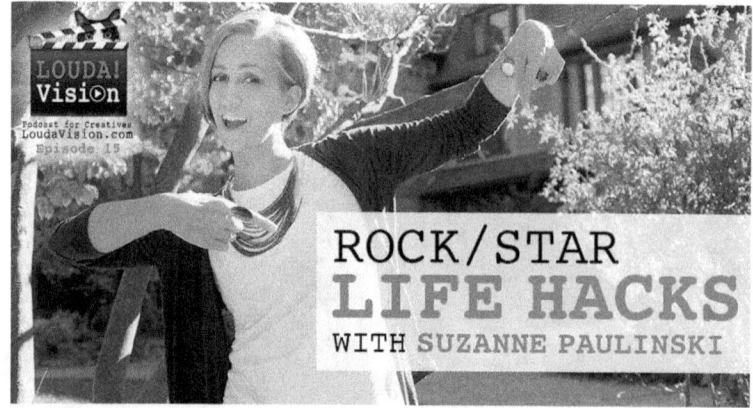

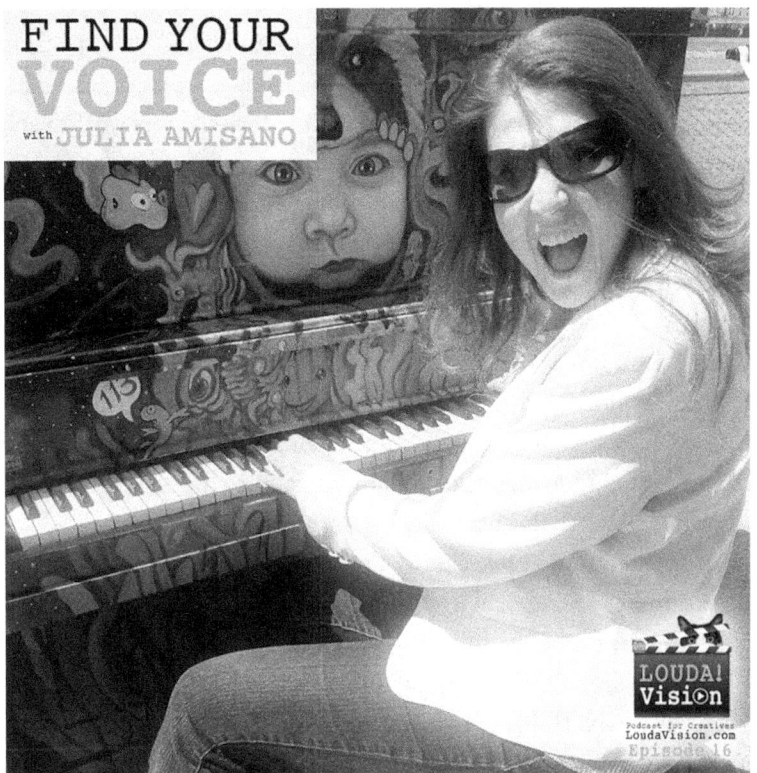

Julia Amisano is a soprano who teaches private voice, piano & acting at her studio in Brooklyn, NY. She is currently working on a reality TV project about her business. Julia has performed in many Operas, Musicals, and Shakespeare plays. She sang at Carnegie Hall every year from 2008-2011 with Remarkable Theatre Brigade's Opera Shorts program. Julia recorded Cassandra's Rant by George Brunner for EMM in 2013 and debuted The Girl From Shunem, w/Metropolitan Opera Tenor Yegishe Manucharyan in 2011. Her classical CD "GREEN" debuted on NPR and is for sale online. She also has an instructional DVD on how to sing called "The Three Pillars of Singing." Julia loves to swing dance, draw and swim. She also loves the seasons and especially loves continuing her steamy affair with New York City whom she adores. www.gracemusicstudiony.com

John Trigonis is a writer, independent filmmaker, TED speaker, and renowned crowdfunding "Zen Master." He has mentored thousands of filmmakers, storytellers, and other creators worldwide to help them craft compelling crowdfunding campaigns that not only reach, but oftentimes exceed their online fundraising goals.

Trigonis also literally wrote and then rewrote the book on Crowdfunding for Filmmakers (now in its second edition) after running his own Indiegogo campaign for his eighth short film Cerise. Through a well-wrought campaign that put to practice his "Three Ps of Crowdfunding" (now his "Three Ways to Let Your Crowd In"), he surpassed his fundraising goal, then enticed his crowd again independent of a platform to raise thousands more to submit Cerise to film festivals.

After spending a few years as a private crowdfunding consultant for a number of creative projects across various platforms, Trigons was brought on board Indiegogo's film team as its Head Film & Creative Campaign Strategist, and he works behind-the-scenes on all of the platform's most successful film and video campaigns like Super Troopers 2, Con Man, Iron Sky: The Coming Race, Code 8, Jodorowsky's Endless Poetry, Dragon's Lair Returns, Miles Ahead, Life Itself, and countless other top-tier films, all while continuing to nurture his own creative multimedia projects. www.johntrigonis.com

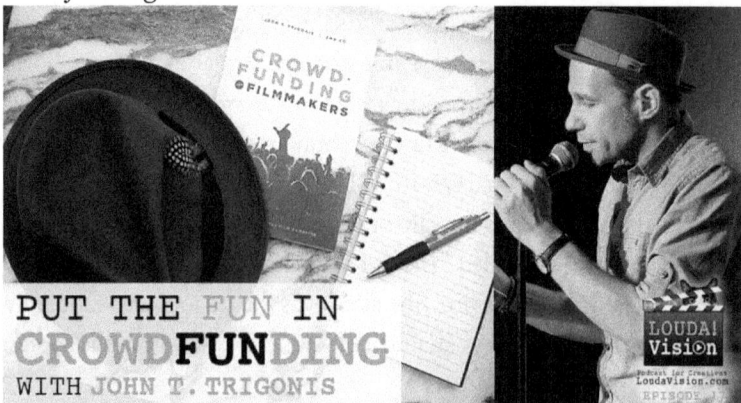

Valentin Farkasch is a Filmmaker and Photographer with family roots in theater and television. After studying Photography in Vienna and working as a TV Camera Operator he moved on to study Cinematography at New York Film Academy which set him on a path to be a full time filmmaker focused on creating digital short form content. When he is not out capturing little moments in time he is watching the slow rise of our robot overlords and is turning his thought about it into a script.

After seven years in NYC, Valentin moved to Austria to pursue a non-creative career. His NYC photography was featured in an exhibit premiere gallery show in 2017 at Dock7. All images are available for sale online. He also launched his own podcast called Creative Ties *(Photo Credit: Nikki Asti)*.
www.ValentinF.com

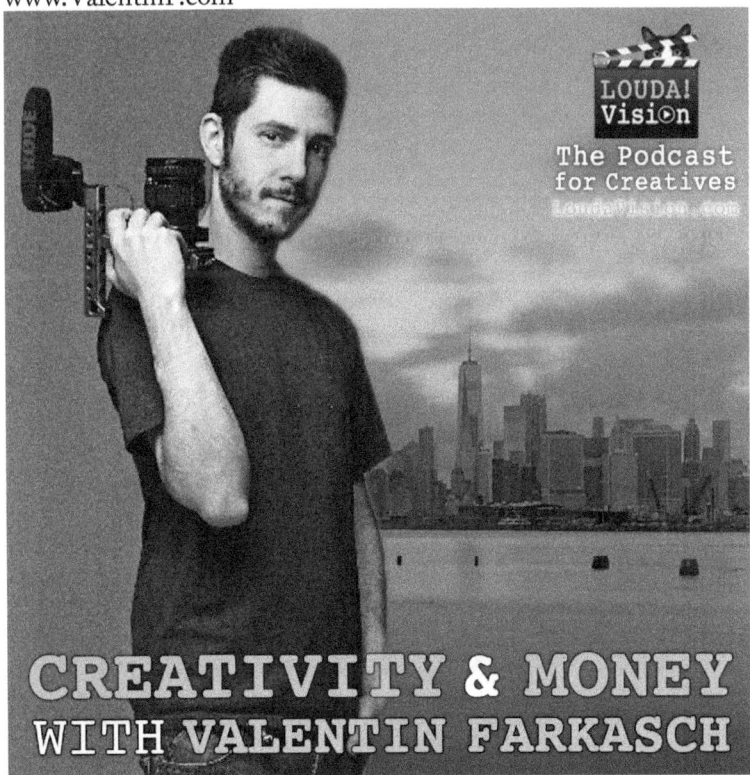

Squeaky Moore describes herself as "One woman, many faces, one creator, many talents." She is regarded as the pitch guru for independent content creators. Having been in the entertainment industry for over 20 years, Squeaky understands the business from every angle. Squeaky is an independent content creator, producer, director, writer, and actress. A mompreneur, she freelances as a development and pitching consultant and strategist. As a writer, director and producer, Squeaky's mission is to enlighten, uplift, and inspire. Squeaky's career path—one designed to artistically address socially conscious issues, invoke discussion for the greater good, to teach and inspire — lies at the very core of who she is, and is continually reflected in her work *(Photo Credit: T'rah Holliday)*.

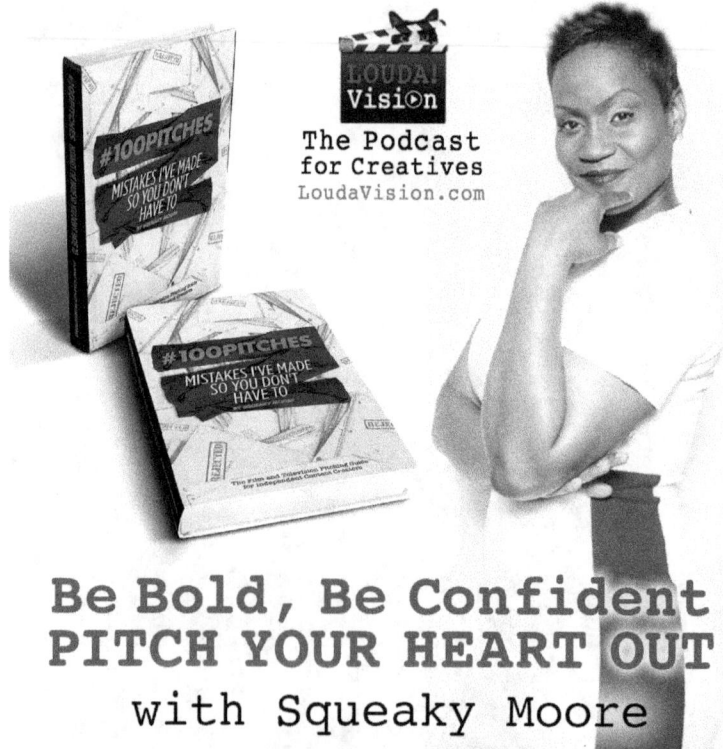

A Chicago native, Squeaky received an MFA from Roosevelt University's Conservatory. A natural storyteller with a "gift for gab," she began using her gifts in 1999, after she created and staged a variety show, "Ack Like U know," which served as catalyst to her starting her production company, Moore Squeaky Productions. She later created an improv-based comedy show, "Guud Timez," based on the 1970's, "Good Times"TV sitcom, followed by staging, "The Ugly Man."

Squeaky moved to New York City to pursue acting but would soon transition into fulfilling her true passion for writing, directing and producing after "64," a project on father absent homes that she produced and assist directed, became a viral sensation. Your Black World described it as 'Life changing and powerful.' On the heels of "64," Squeaky produced, "Father's Day?," a film that addresses the effects of absentee fathers; which debuted on the launch of Magic Johnson's, Aspire TV Network. Some of Squeaky's recent directing and producing credits include, The Positive Controversy," a show in which she developed and is the show-runner, and her latest film project, "Face of Darkness - Journey to Healing," a documentary film that explores depression and suicide in the African American communities.

She recently authored a book for content creators after journeying to pitch her film and television projects 100 times. The book, #100Pitches: Mistakes, I've Made So You Don't Have To, is a film and television pitching guide geared towards independent content creators and about her pitching journey, the do's and don'ts of pitching television and film projects, with interviews from executives in development at networks, and production companies, and independent content creators who have bridged the gap from being independent to the big and small screens. Squeaky is currently on a book-release tour, where she is both workshopping directly from the pages of her book, and, moderating a panel of industry executives in each city she tours.

If you ask Squeaky Moore what is next, she'll tell you, " The sky's the limit." She is currently pitching several projects for television of her own, as well as, developing and pitching projects for others. Squeaky has been featured in Huffington Post, Centric-TV, Madamenoire, Bossip, The Examiner, News One, Amsterdam News, and forecasted a 'woman to watch,' in Ambition Magazine for her work as producer, director and writer. www.thepitch101.com

Teraj is as an accomplished model, brilliant songwriter, social media influencer and gifted dancer. He is a versatile talent who is ready to step into the spotlight as a skillful Pop/R&B singer whose star is certainly on the rise! Born in Miami, Florida on May 25, Teraj grew up with four sisters and three brothers. At a young age, Teraj was enamored by his own creativity, and set his sights high determined to achieve a career in music and performing arts. As a dedicated student at Design & Architecture Senior High (DASH), Teraj participated in a number of stage performances before heading to the prestigious Cornell University, where he earned his Bachelor of Architecture with a Minor in Dance. During his time at Cornell, Teraj was a member of the illustrious a cappella group, The Class Notes, which afforded Teraj the ability to hone in on his vocal skills while participating in the release of promotional singles and tour performances in New York City, Dublin, Paris and Rome. By 2007, Teraj was noted for his exceptional voice and garnered a placement as a bi-weekly resident performer at the Iguana Lounge in midtown Manhattan.

A few years later, fashion photographer Seth London took interest in Teraj after stumbling on the singer's online profile that showcased Teraj's striking features. After a test shoot, London helped develop and guide a modeling career for Teraj that mushroomed into a bona fide profession with Teraj walking NY Fashion Week runway shows and procuring coveted jobs for various brands, including Aeropostale, Calvin Kein, Hermès, YSL and Zara. *(Photo Credit: Seth London)*

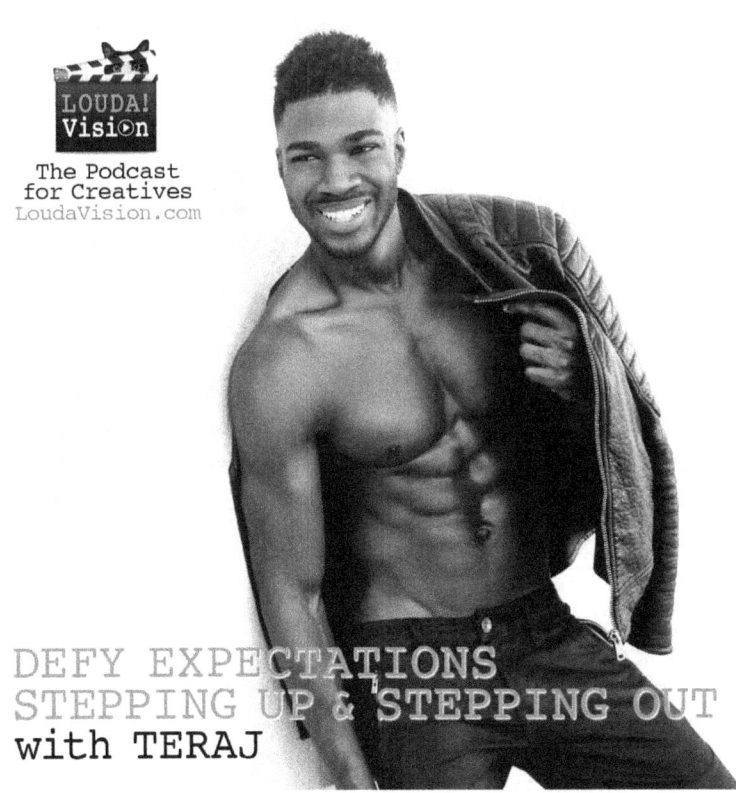

LOUDA!
Visi⊙n
**The Podcast
for Creatives**
LoudaVision.com

DEFY EXPECTATIONS
STEPPING UP & STEPPING OUT
with TERAJ

Teraj's distinct look also helped cast him in numerous music videos such as "23" by Mike Will Made It featuring Miley Cyrus, Wiz Khalifa and Juicy J, and "Stack It Up!" by Meek Mill and Alley Boy. As Teraj gained notoriety for his promising modeling career, in January of 2014, Teraj took on the New York City real estate market as an agent at Keller Williams NYC. And even as a successful real estate agent, Teraj remained in the spotlight, landing more exposure by his appearances on Bravo's hit reality show Million Dollar Listing New York.

In 2016, Teraj returned to his musical roots and started working on his debut album. Through sheer determination, Teraj wrote and produced an eight track EP with songs inspired by chapters of his life, hoping to inspire and uplift his listeners, encouraging them to celebrate humanity through life's splendor and hardships. The album is scheduled for a summer 2017 release, and the lead single "We Got Each Other," already has fans abuzz! With all of his accomplishments, Teraj is just getting started - finally stepping into his own as an entertainer ready to change the world. www.terajmusic.com

Brett Solomano is a stuntman and an author, speaker and coach helping people overcome their fears. Growing up in a small country town (of less than 2000 people!) called Mulwala in New South Wales, Australia, Brett was constantly trying to fight the boredom through riding bikes, jumping out of trees in the local river and watching films. This eventually lead to him making his own short films and getting interested in the stunts he used to watch on tv as a career of his own!

Moving to Melbourne in Victoria, Australia he then continued to pursue his dreams as a stuntman in the TV industry and wrote his first book "A Stuntman's Guide to Learning Anything" and started running workshops on mindfulness, emotional intelligence and overcoming fear for both youth and adults. Continuing his passion as a stuntman and coach, he moved to Los Angeles in 2016 and continues to write for his blog and also spec scripts. He has worked for hundreds of companies in between film jobs, has travelled the world and loves to people watch. He has worked with thousands of clients around the world, including disadvantaged, incarcerated and disabled youth, through to adults stuck in a life they don't want and seeking to follow their dreams and even cancer patients and people with phobias.

Whoever they are, Brett offers them inspiration and guidance toward overcoming their fears on their journey.

(Photo Credit: Karin Schneider Photography)

www.astuntmansguide.com

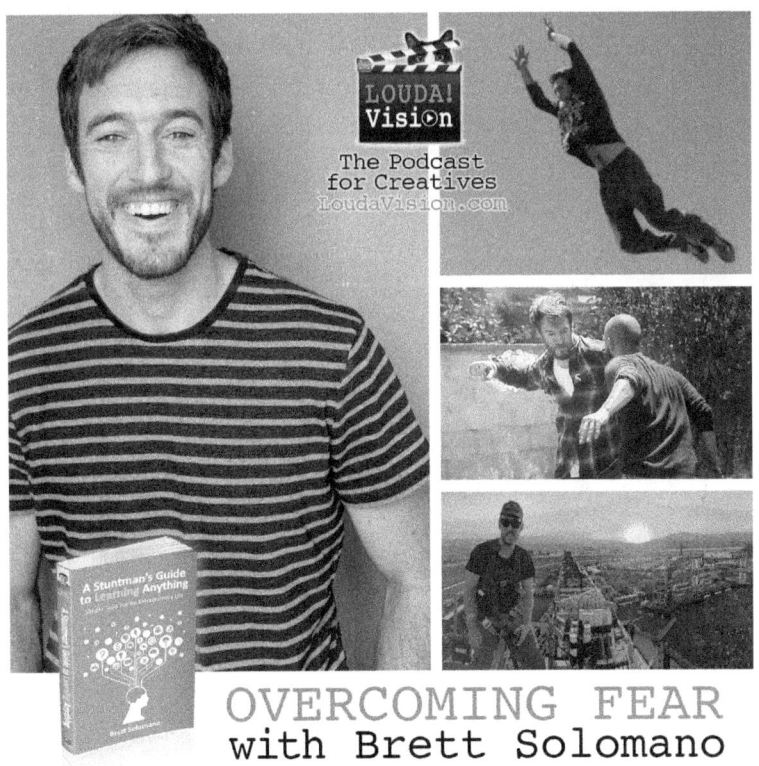

Temica Gross is a best selling author, speaker, budget business coach and founder of Tenacious Purpose Group LLC. An advocate for the purse protective entrepreneur, Temica uses her coaching skills to ignite a spark in each of her clients providing them with the tools and resources they need to build their brands on a BUDGET.

Temica has earned a masters degree in both Human Resource Management (MSHR) and Project Management (MBA) and has worked 10 years in corporate business developing company wide training's and providing creative solutions to company problems. Despite her achievements, Temica knew there was more to life than working the typical 9-5. The spirit of a servant, Temica knows exactly what it feels like to wake up each day with a burning desire to answer the call placed on your life. By using her personal experiences, Temica helps to empower her clients to get out of their OWN way and start where they are! Her unique approach encourages and inspires her clients to develop tailored programs, products and services for their businesses and create greater brand visibility across social media platforms. www.temicagross.com

The Podcast
for Creatives
LoudaVision.com

BUDGET BUSINESS TIPS
with Temica Gross

Magdalena Reilly is an audio-visual media creative who is a passionate environmentalist and minimalist. She was born in Lublin, Poland and has developed her raw personality in the streets of Brooklyn when her family emigrated to America in 1995. Her desire to pursue visual arts was intrigued when she stepped into a darkroom at her high school's photography class. The whole process of photography fascinated her as her biggest influence at the time was Ansel Adams. She studied psychology and film production at Brooklyn College where she endured the love and the hardships of filmmaking. After college instead of following a traditional path she decided to devote a year of her life to AmeriCorps VISTA, in conjunction with the NYC Civic Corps, she was its first graduating cohort in 2010. After it was over, Magdalena was unsure about her "permanent place" in the world and was eager to experience life through travel. She moved to San Diego, California. After working full-time in the field of psychology for three years at various non-profits, it was only in 2015, when the idea of not being able to live without the arts or being able to actively create, shook Magdalena out of a trance of normalcy. With packing her whole life away into storage and selling their car, Magdalena and her husband Joseph Reilly ventured on a three-month journey to Europe. This is where they created a documentary film called "Low White Sky." It focuses on permaculture, vertical farming and urban gardening. After a year of editing the film one creative endeavor led to another, and Magdalena started her podcast about her journey into Minimalism. She currently lives in Eugene, Oregon where she commutes solely by bicycle and is inspired by nature daily to remain open and creative. *(Photo Credit: Joseph Reilly)*
www.MagdalenaReilly.com

MINIMALISM, TRAVEL & DOCUMENTARY FILM
with Magdalena Reilly

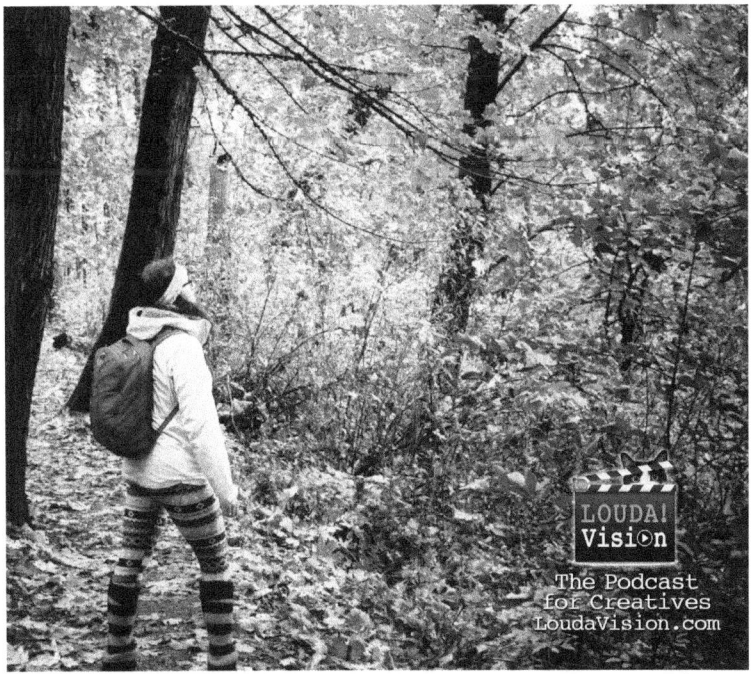

LOUDA!
Visi⊙n

The Podcast
for Creatives
LoudaVision.com

Additional research was conducted as part of a freelance survey I put out in 2017. These answers serve as a way to gain multiple perspectives on the freelance versus full time debate.

Freelance Survey Participants:

Jamal Rolland is a Freelance Video Editor in NYC.
vimeo.com/rocstarvisuals

Alejandro Hernandez is a Freelance Cinematographer & Editor in NYC.
twitter.com/alejandro_mhr

Bryant Coffey is a Freelancer in the Advertising Industry. He lives in San Diego, CA.
www.bryantcoffey.com

Alyscia Cunningham owns a home improvement company. She is also an author, filmmaker and photographer, with a focus on women and social-impact.
www.docsinprogress.nationbuilder.com/hair

Billy Nawrocki is a Freelance Filmmaker & Video Editor in NYC/White Plains.
www.Billynawrocki.com

Diana Cherkas is a Freelance Actor, Writer, Advertising Copywriter & Copy Editor in NYC. @DianaCherkas (on Twitter & Instagram)

Michael Woodward is a Freelance Web Design/Development & Podcast Host in PA and NYC.
www.jumblethink.com

Finally, I will be referencing a never-before-seen interview I did with a professional therapist, which I intended to use as part of a documentary film. Unfortunately the audio from the interview had technical issues. I did not let that setback stop me from utilizing her insights, and so I have included some of her quotes into this book.

Alma Villegas-Schwalbenberg, or **Dr. Alma,** as she is fondly called by her clients, is the President/Founder and the Mover behind AVS Psychological Services, P.C. She has over 15 years of clinical experience working with diverse ages and populations and concurrent 15 years teaching experience in New York City's academic and medical settings.

She has worked with children and adults with developmental disabilities such as cerebral palsy, mental retardation and autism. She specializes in child and family psychotherapy and psychological evaluation with expertise in anxiety and trauma, depression and bereavement. She also has competencies in Management Training and Teacher Training specializing in Needs Analysis and Team Building. She has also served at Albert Einstein School of Medicine/Bronx Lebanon Hospital as a faculty member teaching medical residents and psychiatry fellows.

Dr. Alma has 10 years experience in cross-cultural training, starting as a Project Director with the Peace Corps/Philippines and currently holds the position of Psychologist-in-Residence and Cross-Cultural Advisor to the IPED (International Political Economic Development) Graduate Program of Fordham University. www.visionofself.com

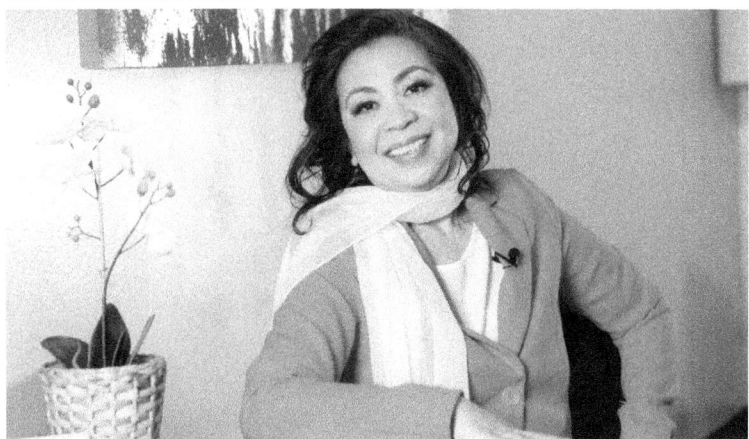

CHAPTER 1

LEARNING THE SAME LESSON, AGAIN AND AGAIN

It seems we always learn the most important lessons over and over again until it sticks.

When I graduated from high school, I wanted to study film production at Brooklyn College. However, I didn't have the courage to tell anyone that I wanted to major in something so risky. When you major in accounting, for example, there is a clear idea of what you will be doing for money after you graduate. A career in Hollywood Film and Television is less clear, and it seems like an unattainable dream for most. It is a competitive industry because it seems so glamorous and easy. Just pick up a camera or write a story, and BOOM, you're a filmmaker. Believe me, it is NOT that easy, but it has moments when it is an extremely rewarding career choice.

Thinking back on it now, I didn't believe that I could achieve this goal. The biggest hurdle for me at the time was so short sighted: my commute to Brooklyn College was a two hour train ride, each way. I wasn't ready for that commitment as an 18 year old, and I didn't believe in myself. I was my own biggest critic, always have been, always will be.

Instead, I took liberal arts classes at a closer college, and fulfilled all of the English prerequisites for a journalism major in my freshman year. I loved going to this college and it is where I met one of my best friends. The only problem was that I hated journalism. I didn't realize this until I took the official class for it. This might sound surprising seeing as how you're reading a book that I wrote. It wasn't the act of writing that I hated, or interviewing people, it was all the rules and formatting that felt so rigid and lacking creativity. Writing articles sucked the joy out of the process for me. I am a storyteller today in many ways: my podcast, video productions, this book, and whatever other creative projects come next. At that moment in time, journalism (in the newspaper sense) wasn't right for me. I realized that I needed to follow my dream of going to film school at Brooklyn College. After I graduated with my Bachelor's degree in Film & TV Production, I was in talks to work at my favorite TV network. Walking into that dream network, I felt so proud of my hard work. I felt as if I had made it, and this would be my forever job. Two months later though, I knew it wasn't for me. I am a dedicated worker, I am passionate and creative, and I am ambitious. What I am NOT, is a brown-noser, so the tradition of newbies at that company working 12-hour days just to impress the bosses, with no opportunities to have hands-on training; it never felt right to me. I work quickly and efficiently, and will never dumb down or slow down my work to show that I'm the first person in the office, and the last one to leave. I prefer to work somewhere that promotes based on experience and skill, not just seniority. I learned what works for me, and what doesn't based on my personality and work ethic. I learned that it is more important to know myself, than to mold my personality to fit a job. I tell you this story to show that I learned this lesson twice in the span of four years, over 10 years ago, and I am still learning that lesson today.

In early 2017, I was six years into my tenure as a multimedia producer and editor at a college. This job was very comfortable because of the great people I worked with. It also had cushy benefits that kept me there, and I was there long enough to learn this important lesson. When offered a higher paying, higher title job at another college, I optimistically jumped ship and left my comfort zone. After a few short weeks I realized that this new job was not right for me. My health was suffering, the commute sucked, I seriously lacked work-life balance, and this was not the job where I could use my biggest asset, my creativity.

So I quit. Life is short. Why waste precious time somewhere that isn't right for me?

Let me disclaimer this story by saying I am not rich, but I do have some money saved for emergencies, and I had been building my freelance client list for more than five years. It was not a huge risk to quit this new job, but it was very scary. For the first time in seven years, I was unemployed.

But let's not use that word, unemployed. I decided to use this experience to finally experiment with freelancing as a full time career. In my comfort zone, I would never have taken this leap.

First thing I did was reach out to all the part time gigs that I was doing on the side. Just a month earlier, I had told them I was unavailable when I got that new job. Now, I made a declaration that I am available and looking for work, no scheduling restrictions. I also passed along my new and improved resume to them, so they could see how I would be able to contribute to their team.

Applying to jobs and putting out feelers to your network is impossible though, if you don't know what you're looking for. After a long time working for one employer, it can be easy to look for that same comfortable thing again and again. But then, we would be stuck in the same situation we were trying to break out of. The lesson that I keep learning over and over again in my career, is that it is very important to learn what you DON'T WANT, even more so than what you do.

During my freelance experiment, I expected to be working for myself. However, I quickly realized that when you don't have a steady paycheck coming in, there is less of a decision to make when a paying project comes along. Since there is no steady income, every potential gig is one that I have to take. Also, there is always someone to report to, because there is always someone writing that check or sending the payment. The person with the money is who I work for. If I'm not paying myself, I'm not working for myself. There is always a client or a boss and as a freelancer I am constantly providing services in exchange for income.

Entrepreneurship is an option for people who want to do it all, and have the capability to wear multiple hats. While I am a great multitasker, I prefer to stay on the creative side and I like to constantly collaborate with others. Therefore entrepreneurship might not exactly be the perfect path for me. We will discuss the difference between entrepreneurship and freelancing in the next chapter.

In the meantime, I can tell you how I spent my time as a freelancer. I have become an expert in my field, learned to brand myself and grow my own creative project: the LoudaVision Podcast (and this book). I have used this time to discover the most effective way to network, master the art of job hunting and interviewing, learning how to maintain a positive mindset and identify my long term career goals after years of feeling lost and confused. I have gained confidence to know that I don't need a full time job. If one comes along that is perfect for me, I will consider it, but I don't need it. I have turned my mindset from lacking, to abundance and gratitude, giving me clarity. This book will help you achieve some of these same goals and give you the knowledge to decide for yourself what is right for you, and what isn't.

There are many ways to make money in today's economy. As a creative genius YOU have the talent and ambition to achieve your goals. Without clarity though, we are running on a treadmill to nowhere. I encourage you to use my story, and the stories mentioned in this book, as a way to look inward at your own experiences and feelings so you can identify your own recurring lessons.

I am not encouraging you to dwell on the past or to define

yourself by your failures. I am asking you to look at those experiences with fresh eyes, without judgement and using your creative skills to grow from that. Take all of the good and bad from your past experiences, and create a Frankenstein of your ideal future career.

It's easy for us to realize when we don't feel good, or if something doesn't feel right to us. In this book, I will help you identify those moments of gut wrenching unhappiness and look back at your career to see patterns that give you the keys to your ideal future. Those bad jobs are so important. Any negative person or bad mood can take a happy moment and find the worst in it. At the same time, the most positive person can identify when something does NOT feel good. It's much easier to notice a gut feeling of dread or unhappiness, than it is to realize we are actually happy. After all, feeling good is all about our mindset. We can be happy even in bad situations, or looking back at bad occurrences. It's all about perspective.

CHAPTER 2

PROTECT YOUR PERSPECTIVE

I am the daughter of an Italian-American lower-middle class family. My father was born here in the United States, and my mother born in Italy and emigrated here as a child. I mention that because their generation believed in the American dream. Their ultimate goal was to find a job that can afford them a house and a family. What that job was- is not too important, so long as it makes them money. That is success.

When I left my easy breezy job for a management position at a prestigious college, making more money than I had ever made, I know that my parents were really proud of me. When I decided to give that position up, my initial thought, even though I am an adult, was that they would think I'm a failure. I feared what people at my last job would think. I feared that my husband would think I'm a quitter and that I'm irresponsible. We all judge each other, but if we're always worried about what others think of us, we'll never truly do anything for ourselves. Truth is, people don't really think about others for too long. Even if they are judging me, could it be any worse than the self-judgement I put upon myself?

I considered keeping this move a secret, until I realized that my future depended heavily on my network and the people around me. I also made a promise to myself years ago that I would never lie to my family. It is important to me that I live up to those values I hold for myself. It was difficult to tell my parents about this decision, but I was pleasantly surprised by the accepting response. This lesson taught me to care less about what others think and encouraged me to live as an honest person. Here's a bit more about perspective from Dr. Alma Villegas-Schwalbenberg. In an interview I conducted with her, she spoke about her parent's perspective regarding work:

> *"They did it to provide for us materially for the home, to send the kids to school was their legacy. So work is a means to achieving goals. For myself, work is an expression of my own self, of course it's nice to have money to spend for your child's schooling but it also has to be meaningful work. I have to love my job to be effective."*

This shift in generational perspectives when it comes to work is not uncommon. For a lot of us, our parents and grandparents emigrated to the United States in search of the "American Dream." That dream oftentimes meant working long hours in a factory or a manual labor job to make money that would put food on their table. Their dream was to buy a house, get a car, to provide for their children. Today we are seeing that the average college graduate is buried in student loan debt and homeownership is an unattainable goal for many because of the rising cost of real estate. Back in the late 1980's, my parent's house cost them as much as it would cost me to buy a car today. With such a huge difference in expenses, home-ownership is not on the radar for a lot of young people.

Knowing that we have such a huge hurdle to jump just to attain the same things our parents did, it is no surprise that our goals have changed. Working forty hours at a minimum wage job will likely not get us a house, let alone get us out of debt any time soon. So why spend most of our waking hours at a job that doesn't make us happy? Our relationship to work has changed.

"How do we define work, or does your work define you? We fall into the trap of intertwining our identity with work. That's why we have workaholics- it's easy to feel good because we see something tangible. Of course the more work you do, the more successful you find your work, the more you are drawn to work. How do we find the happiness in the work? It's how do we change our attitude- how do we see our work? If we see our work as paying our bills and doing fun stuff with our family versus this [laborious] work- what is my meaningful contribution? Am I helping the economy? Am I making a difference with my coworkers? How do I fit into this scenario- am I one of them or am I untouched knowing my true worth and trying to under-stand my role in the here and now of the situation? So a lot has to do with being able to see the intangible results of work. What is happening inside of us at work? What is happening to fellow workers because I am there? That you cannot measure. You can only measure the boss saying 'good job', or if you accomplish this [task]. The intangible and tangible and be aware of the benefits for our own growth."
-Alma Villegas-Schwalbenberg, PHD

If we can keep our perspective in-check and separate our identity from our job, then perhaps that is the key to happiness. It seems like Alma is saying our parents were right, but not exactly. My theory is that we have to love our work in order to be happy, but have a separation in our identity to know that we are not defined by our work. This way, if an article we write is mercilessly marked up in red for changes, we don't have to hate our boss or think we are a failure. We can identify that we did our best in writing that article, and that since we are getting paid for our work, it is simply an exchange of services for us to accept criticism and revise our work to fit their preferences. We do not have to take it personally.

We are not our work, but we can still love what we do and be proud of what we accomplish.

This separation starts when we realize that we have control over the thoughts in our mind, the same way we control the movements in our body. The thoughts in our mind are created by us. If we don't like what's being said in there, good news- we are the director, writer and actor of those thoughts. We can make revisions.

As a teenager, I used to be sad at night. No matter how many people I had with me during the day, it's that silent moment when my head hits the pillow, where I would feel most lonely. Today, I think of this quiet moment before sleep as empowering! Even though I have my husband next to me physically, I am still the only one inside my head. The last thoughts I have to hear before sleep, are my own. My mind is the only place I can go and be completely silent. Some people, like me, turn to God in moments like this. To each his own.

Whether you spend these quiet moments praying, meditating, or something else, you are still in your mind speaking to yourself. I choose to tell myself positive things, and to think about what I am grateful for, not just on Thanksgiving, but every day. I choose healthy thoughts for myself, and that has improved my relationship with ME. Now, being alone is not lonely because I am a positive person to be around. I have built confidence by being kind to myself, and because I see how I have power and control over my own thoughts.

I do not believe there is one single solution to make every person happy all the time. Even my gratitude and meditation practice has moments where it does not work for me. We each have to have an individual, specific plan for those moments of sadness. Only you can decide what it is that can pull you out of that negativity. Just know that negativity, like positivity, is a choice. You are in control.

"Defeating my negative voice has been done by visualizing a James Bond positive voice that's on my right shoulder. [On

the left shoulder] This Sméagol, gross, ET, gremlin-looking figure... you can just kick him. Once you kick him in the pig pen, he knows his role. He hides behind a black smoke... Negativity is illogical because you can literally make up positive things and say them to yourself instead. A worry is worrying about a future event that hasn't happened, that will happen in a negative way. You've got to speak your belief [and desires] into the universe and it becomes that much more real. You've got to let it out of your head and you've got to speak it. That's going to commit you to take the next baby step, that next actionable thing to get out of the pit of whether it's an injury bringing you down, or whatever it is."
-Jacob Bacaner: Entrepreneur,
Fitness Model & Coach

Even if you are not yet well-versed in positive thinking, that's okay. Find a positive voice that you relate to, even if it's not your own. There are tons of motivational speakers, spirituality practices and self-help techniques out there. Find the one that works for you, and know that every single thought is a choice. Just because you make one bad choice, there are infinite opportunities to change that mindset at any moment.

Of course, it's really hard to not let someone else's negative comments crap all over your positive perspective. If we are caught off guard, even a stranger can make us feel bad about ourselves.

My first ever networking event was a huge lesson for me. It was an event for fellow filmmakers and my mindset going in was that I should try to impress others. This was a mistake. I was asked the usual question "So, what do you do?"

Now picture me at the event talking about my films, my podcast... I even had a wing-woman who insisted on throwing my Emmy-win into the conversation. All of a sudden this random stranger cuts me off and says... *"Whoa! That's too many things! I'll never remember you. You have to tell me ONE thing about you that I can remember, otherwise, NEXT!"*

I wish I could tell you that I had a witty response for her in that moment, but I didn't. I backtracked. I felt small and defensive. She got to me.

Looking back at it as someone who always has a better response AFTER the situation, I realize that I don't have to simplify who I am for anyone, ever. You never know when you might be in a situation with a strong-willed, confident person who's telling YOU how to be YOU.

My mindfulness meditation practice helps keep me grounded in who I truly am inside. I set my intention before each potentially stressful situation. It's a mini-self-pep-talk, reminding me that I don't have to impress anyone. I don't have to be liked. It's not a competition.

At the next event, rather than try to impress others, I put that overwhelming objective out of my mind. As a journalist, my approach was to ask questions and find out about other people. I did not talk about myself unless they asked, or unless it was relevant to what they brought up. This revised approach to networking helps me in every single small talk situation. After all, people love talking about themselves, and I love hearing people's stories. This was how I connected to who I truly am, and used that part of myself to connect with others in a deeper way.

I am very shy when meeting new people, and sometimes finding an appropriate ice breaker question is really hard. A quick trick I learned is to pay a genuine compliment to the person you are meeting. It could be their shoes, their nails, smile, or even a comment on how delicious their drink looks- followed by a question about that thing. It feels good to be kind to people, and in turn they let down their guard.

"Compliments are your currency. It's free currency. No

matter how broke you are, you could always give someone a compliment, whether it's a homeless person that just needs someone to act like a brother for a minute of his day. Or if it's someone who looks really sad on the train. You never know, their girlfriend or boyfriend may have dumped them that day. We've all been in that heartbreak and we know what that feels like. We're all a big family, brothers and sisters. When you walk by strangers, that's you in a year or two, if you judge them. Sometimes, not always, it's not to scare you, but I always find that whenever I judge someone accidentally, if it just pops into my head, BOOM. All of a sudden, a year later, I'm sitting in the same situation."

-Jacob Bacaner: Entrepreneur,
Fitness Model & Coach

We will have to attend a lot of networking events and social gatherings in our life. These are great opportunities to practice your positive perspective and ability to connect. Get in the right mindset before walking in that door, and you will have put the armor on to protect yourself from all the potential negativity that will come your way.

The people we surround ourselves with are another choice that we have control over. You may have heard the expression, "If you're the smartest person in the room, you're in the wrong room." I live by this saying, and use it to constantly push myself beyond my comfort zone. Don't be fooled into thinking that we only have to network with and befriend people our own age, or in our own zip code. Thanks to the internet, our circle of friends is limitless and we have unlimited ways to connect with people.

If you are traveling, make a plan to meet locals, and learn from them. Every day there can be an opportunity to connect with others and learn something from them. Often times people who are more accomplished than us will have great advice that we might want to follow. Sometimes we can see their success as inspiration for which we aspire to. For example, on a recent trip to Atlanta, my husband and I coordinated a time to meet with my mentor's sister, Helena. She has a great job at a prestigious college and is at retirement age, but loves to work so much that she isn't stopping anytime soon. We toured the college where she works and my husband learned a great deal about the new field of work he is studying. He also met a lot of people in his industry, as she introduced him and gave him the opportunity to ask questions.

Even though this trip was planned as a benefit to him, I also learned a lot about myself. Being on campus again made me miss working for a college, and reminded me about all the things I love about a career in academia. Since this trip, I was able to identify my chosen field of study and have decided to get my Master's degree in Learning and Instructional Technology. This is not too far off from my past experience and interests, but seeing Helena so happy with her chosen career- made me realize that I have the potential to be happy as well. It reminded me that we have the ability to create a career we actually enjoy. There is no amount of money in the world that can make us happy. Money and happiness are on two separate spectrums. The definition of success is not a dollar amount, it is immeasurable.

We can channel happiness using perspective. We can gain success through achieving our goals. We can achieve our goals by making meaningful connections with people. So aside from meeting people in our everyday life, there are networking events that are organized exactly for this purpose. However, there isn't enough time in the world to attend all of the events in our area. Choose the networking events you attend wisely. They should be relevant to your career or personal goals, and not cost more money than you can comfortably afford. I personally do not like spending money on networking events because for me, 90% of the people I meet at these events do not become clients. Sometimes I will make a friend though, and that is valuable in it's own way. I am experimenting over the next few months with going to paid events to test a theory. Perhaps going to free events attracts people who are not willing to pay for things. That mindset could be exactly the reason I have such a low client conversion rate at the moment. Surely I will keep investigating this as it is an important part of being an entrepreneur and a freelancer.

Something important I've learned about networking events, is that I am more successful when I am the only one of ME in a room. As a filmmaker, I quickly learned that I am not going to make money or a lasting impression on anyone, by going to networking events with other filmmakers. It was fun and nice to meet like-minded people, but no one was going to hire me because everyone there can do the same thing that I can do. We often spent time talking shop and didn't have many opportunities to offer each other because essentially we were each other's competition.

I started attending events for local business owners, and that's when I became the hot commodity. I met people who needed my services. By attending a small business event in your local area, you have a chance to meet people who might actually need your services because they don't know how to do what you do. They need you and you need them. These are the best types of networking events to attend. Do not be afraid to stand out in a room full of people for being the youngest, or least educated, or the only one of you. Your unique qualities and interests are an advantage, they make you interesting. Use every opportunity to meet someone new as a chance to learn something and make a friend. Don't go into it with the intention of selling.

> *"I am terrible at asking people for jobs or listing my accomplishments to impress people. They say everyone is a potential client, and while that's possibly true, I can't approach life that way."*
> *-Diana Cherkas: Freelance Actor, Writer,*
> *Advertising Copywriter & Copy Editor*

The key to maximize your potential income as a freelancer is to specialize in multiple areas, and be able to pull out the relevant example of your expertise in the right situation. Remember when I was speaking about networking events? I met a woman who was confused by my multiple roles and insisted that I narrow myself down to one thing so she can remember me. People like that are trying to make you feel small, and you should never define yourself or minimize your worth to impress someone. She did have a point though. Because I was attending a networking event with people who are other freelancers in my field, it was not a place where we could offer anything to each other.

Once you identify and attend the correct networking events with potential clients, listen for what they need, and how you can help. This is not the best time to overwhelm them with all the great things you do, although at times someone who is truly interested might hear the relevant information and ask you more about that. It's not likely they are listening past the first sentence of what you do. Therefore, we want to ask them questions about what they do, and actually listen for a response. In a way, you will be listening for what you can offer them, and providing them the specific information they need about you.

For example, if someone has an event they need recorded, I could mention a recent event that I filmed. Now they know that I specialize in event videography. The same thing can be done for marketing videos, or teaching, or podcasting. Hear how they need help and offer them a solution even if you are not the right person for the job. If it's not something in your wheelhouse, maybe you have a friend you could suggest. People will remember you for how you can help them. Even if they don't need anything right now, they might in the future. When you are looking to make money providing services that you specialize in, you have to be able to communicate that experience and your value to others. Let them know how you can help. Similarly, you might have your own project that needs funding, it is the same thing. Let them know how they can help you.

"I'm talking as a creative, I'm just as much creative as anything else. I think there is no difference when it comes to crowd-funding. If you want an investor, you can get an investor. Everybody is looking to give money to something. You just gotta have some contacts. Then you have to be a little bit of a business person. You have to put on the mask and be like, 'I'm passionate. This is a great project.' Button up your shirt and tie and then be like, 'Here's my plan of how we're going to make money for you'. That world, yes, you have to do that."
-John T. Trigonis: Filmmaker, Poet & Indiegogo's
Head Film and Creative Campaign Strategist

For some, self-promotion and networking is not natural, and that's okay. Some people, but not everyone you meet will be impressed by you. It's more likely your business card will be thrown in the trash before someone follows up with you. Don't have expectations of strangers. It's like hoping for the best but preparing for the worst. You will be pleasantly surprised and grateful for an authentic connection. If you don't make a connection, then nothing was lost.

If a friend, relative or coworker is not encouraging you, or is making you feel bad about yourself- it is your choice to keep associating with them. It really is simple. Get the toxic people out of your life if you want to be happy and successful. Even the most talented person, if they have a bad attitude, can end up with no future. It's hard enough for us to keep our own mind positive. We shouldn't have to worry about cheering up someone else. Surely we all have encountered energy vampires in our life. As a creative person, the most common vampire for me is someone who wants to always ask my professional opinion on a creative idea they have, but they likely have no intention of following through on that idea. Even strangers approach me for this type of advice, requesting a consultation to decide if they want to work with me. These type of people usually do not have any intention of paying for anything. They just want to talk and have someone to listen. At times they will take the ideas you've contributed to the conversation and use it as encouragement to actually execute their project. In those cases, great. I am happy to spark someone's creativity and lend an alternate form of thinking that will help them achieve. Remember that a vampire sucks your blood for their own nourishment. We're not getting eternal life (or anything, actually) from energy vampires in our life, so it's up to us to protect our gifts from those who do not value our time. If you are spending more time talking through someone else's project with them, then you are spending on your own career or creative endeavors, then maybe it's time to reassess how much you can give to this person. It might sound cold, but we can't always say YES to everyone else, if that means saying NO to ourselves.

Those same people might want to hear your creative ideas and encourage you to talk about them. If so, great, but if they are negatively influencing you or making you feel bad about your efforts, it's time to cut them off. I am not talking about constructive criticism-that is very valuable and necessary for growth. I'm speaking of people who want to hear your ideas so they can tell you all the reasons why they would not do that, or point out all the difficulties of that endeavor. Cut those people off. Only ask for constructive criticism from people who you trust to be honest (even if the truth hurts) and people who have accomplished something similar, who have expertise in that subject. It's easy to mistake a know-it-all, overly confident person for someone who is accomplished. Always check resumes and references. This could mean scoping out someone's LinkedIn page, or taking an interest in their work.

In some situations, we might not want to cut off a family member or might not be able to cut off a coworker. In that case, just remember that you don't have to tell everyone everything about yourself. Keep big plans a secret if it makes you feel better. Similarly, social media is for friends. If you are working with people who are not supportive of your life outside of work, or people who judge what you do, you don't have to befriend them on social media. This is your choice. Choose wisely.

Sometimes people are not negative, but feel they are being encouraging by giving unsolicited advice. It's funny when those people are giving advice about something they have not succeeded at in their own life. If you have a plan to go back to school, switch careers, start a new creative project, whatever it is, make your plans for yourself after research and consideration. Don't let others decide for you. This advice could be disguised as a barrage of critical questions. Don't be fooled. Not everyone has your best interest at heart, and not everyone is an expert. Be careful who you solicit advice from.

> *"You've got to trust yourself and trust your own intelligence. Only you know what you should take in baby steps every day towards a larger, grander vision of yourself where you have a big mansion, a Maserati and a big foyer. Trust yourself. Only you know what you want to do."*
> *—Jacob Bacaner: Entrepreneur,*
> *Fitness Model & Coach*

If we live by other people's standards, we fail. We can never live up to another person's dreams. So from life coaches, to friends, to that nosy relative who insists on telling you what you should be doing with your life... Stop clinging to other people for permission to try things. It is okay to fail or give up at something that isn't working. It's okay to try new things. It's okay to change your mind. It's okay to live YOUR life the way you want.

CHAPTER 3

YOU CAN QUIT YOUR JOB TODAY

When is it really time to quit our day job? That job we hate, that we drag ourselves to 5 or more days per week. That job that feels so insignificant in the grand scheme of life. We spend more of our lives at this job, than with the people we actually love.

First, I want to note that no job is perfect. There are minor annoyances and stresses that will occur every day, even in a job we otherwise love. How do we determine if our job is worth it?

I will provide you with both positive and negative aspects of quitting your job, so you can make the most informed decision possible. Of course there is nothing more effective than to just try something for yourself. If you can, quit, or take a temporary leave of absence, and see where life takes you.

Some of us don't have the luxury of doing this. We might have a lot of financial responsibilities, people who depend on us, etc. In this situation where we cannot just quit, it's best to analyze what we dislike about our current job. Keep reading to know the possibilities, but use the assignments coming up to think about how you can make small changes to your current position, that might increase your satisfaction. The reality is that everyone's financial situation and responsibilities are different. What works for one might not work for all. Possible solutions if you absolutely cannot afford to leave your job, could be transferring to a different department or trying for a promotion. However, in sticking with our positive mindset, I do not want you to assume that you cannot leave your current job. Life has seasons of ups and downs. If you are working at a job you hate, and it is too far gone to resolve, it's time for YOU to make an up.

Do you have confidence in your own ability? Do you believe that you will succeed even if you don't have a steady income? Do you believe you will do anything to survive?

The answer should be YES.

Whether or not you're going to do it- Believe that you CAN quit your job, so you have the power to make a choice.

I spent a long time complaining about the job I hated, and all the reasons why. No one likes complainers- I'm sure I pissed off a lot of people. I spent years here knowing it was wrong for me, interviewing for other jobs that were also not right for me. In fact, I turned down three full time job offers in that last year. I was stuck. I was dissatisfied. Even after getting a promotion, I soon found myself unhappy all over again. At first, I thought something was wrong with ME. All these perfectly good jobs that other people would kill to have, and I was turning them down. It was affecting my self-image, affecting my home life, and making me lose confidence in my own abilities.

I accepted a job offer for something very similar, but a higher title, higher pay, and longer commute. After just one month of working at what I thought was my dream job, I realized it was not right for me. It wasn't the amount of responsibility, or the people, or the work that was not right. It was the culture, and the lack of work-life balance that I could not commit to any longer. This might sound familiar from the last chapter, but that is because it seems to happen to me again and again. The only difference was that this time, when it repeated, I changed my response. I didn't look for another job and jump right back in.

Since May, I have been working as a freelancer to grow my digital media production business. Part of that includes expanding from just video production, into "digital media" such as graphics and social media. However, I have noticed the most demand for video editing (which is my specialty). It has been liberating to commit myself to more teaching assignments, including one on one tutoring, and group training. I am even discussing the possibility of teaching at a one of the most prestigious workshop facilities in NYC. Opportunities really opened up when I stopped limiting myself based on a preconceived notion- that I have to work a full time job.

However, freelancing comes with a whole new set of personal challenges. For one, I have always been pretty modest, and do not feel comfortable speaking about my accomplishments. I also do not feel comfortable being a sales-person. Yet, freelancing is all about selling yourself. It's about pitching and discussing the possibility of working together with everyone you possibly can.

I truly feel that everything I have done up to this point has prepared me for this freelance experiment. I am grateful for my two-year journey of creating a TV series, which helped me study the pitching process. This includes a podcast interview I did with pitch expert Squeaky Moore in which I learned how to make connections with people I otherwise would not be able to meet. I also took a class at the School of Visual Arts in which I learned how to pitch myself and my TV series. While it is not fun or comfortable to pitch myself, it is a necessary part of being an entrepreneur. If you are not promoting yourself, no one else will. That includes sending cold e-mails to strangers, mentioning what you can offer whenever possible, and attending networking events.

Even harder than pitching is convincing potential clients that what I can give them is worth paying for. In this digital age, logos (for example) are being offered for free or even $5 on these sites that provide cookie-cutter services from producers overseas who have very low living expenses. Oftentimes, what they are providing to their clients is a template, or stock photo, and you can find a dozen other logos that look exactly the same. The challenge for me becomes, how do I inform people of the value they are getting from a local professional?

Some people just don't have the budget for a pro, and that's fine. What I'm learning is that money is not the only thing that is a valued commodity for me. Barter (if it's something I can use) is definitely an option. Some jobs pay hourly, some are project based, and some only offer "exposure." For young professionals with little experience in their field, exposure can be invaluable. Depending on your experience level, it is up to you to decide if you can work for lesser pay just to get exposure. It is not okay to work for free though. Doing this only cheapens your craft, and you are taking money away from other professionals in your industry.

Most of all I'm learning to become flexible in the services I offer so that I can meet people at their price point. I'm expanding my knowledge-base by learning new things and taking on projects that are not what I'm used to. In later chapters, we will discuss how you can discover what unique talents you have to offer, and how to obtain relevant training to expand your knowledge-base.

My goal as a freelancer, at first, was to make the same monthly income that I was making at my last job. It was not hard to meet that goal once I started letting my network know that I am available. The next step for me is exceeding that goal. So far there have been stellar months, and others where I did not come close that goal. In the months that are not so great, it's hard to stay positive. It's tough to stay committed to something that doesn't look like it's working. The thing to remember about freelance life is that you cannot measure its success the same way you measured your 9-to-5. In a traditional job, you are paid a certain salary per year, or per hour, or per week. You pretty much know how much money you are taking home each month, in exchange for the set schedule you are required to work. Throw out that expectation. You cannot measure freelancing in the same way.

Freelancing is living by the seat of your pants. It's not knowing what next week's schedule is going to look like, sometimes not even tomorrow. It's spending countless hours bidding on jobs out of anxiety because next month's calendar is LITERALLY blank. This is my biggest struggle- fear of the unknown.

The most liberating part of freelancing is realizing that every hour of my day is potential income. I am no longer sitting in what feels like detention (AKA a full time job) just waiting for the clock to reach 5pm. As a freelancer or contractor, I only get paid for the hours I work. The faster I do my work, the more time I have for new money-making projects, and the more time I have to enjoy life. This can be a liberating realization, or I could look at it as potentially lessening my opportunity for free-time. It's all about perspective. Your mindset is the most important part of successful freelancing. Mindset is what makes me "an entrepreneur" rather than "unemployed."

While my freelance experiment is still somewhat new, I know that the best thing I ever did for myself was to quit the job that was making me unhappy. I spent too many years of peeking over the fence at the green, beautiful grass that some call "working for yourself."

Here's the reality: short of winning the lottery, you will likely always be working for someone else. As a freelancer I have more bosses, more clients and more meetings than I did when I was a full time employee. I work more hours and don't get payed consistently. I also have more responsibilities since I am now a business owner, and I don't have an HR department to do my paperwork. There are ways to mitigate the stress of working for others, but overall, it will always come with some level of difficulty.

Others might attach a negative stigma to us if we admit that we hate working for other people. Stop caring what other people think about you. The followers in life who like to just live by the status quo, will dismiss us as being disagreeable, as being lazy or unrealistic. Those are the people who will always be working for someone else happily, with little to no growth in their lives, with small expectations of what they could become. This is not necessarily a bad way to live. They will always be more happy and satisfied than we are, and that means they have won at life. They are successful. They are better off than we are. They are winning because they do not let their own ideas make them feel small. They are happy no matter what the external circumstances of their lives may be. They are happy because they do not define themselves by their career.

But that's not what you expected to hear, is it? It's easy to bash followers, or easy-going people for being weak or complacent. It's that very complacency that makes them happier than we are. Instead of judging, let's borrow from them. Let's adopt their vision of themselves, and how they put their ego aside to just complete tasks without emotional connection. How do they not let other people's critique of their work affect who they are? Answer- they don't take it as a personal attack. This is easier said than done, I know.

In episode 2 of the LoudaVision, my guest Anahita Moghaddam speaks about her philosophy as a buddhist and spiritual coach. She challenges us to think about what we need in order to achieve our goals.

> *"I would challenge anyone to go within and find what is the most conducive inner environment you need to make the art you want to make, rather than think it's going to be some kind of external circumstances that will allow that art to be made."*
> *-Anahita Moghaddam: Mindfulness*
> *Coach & Speaker, Neural Beings*

For me, I love freelancing because I am in charge of my own schedule. I can get up from my chair, stretch out my stiff back and go to the gym mid-day if I want, because I am the boss. I am not glued to a seat for eight hours straight. I can flow with my own bursts of creativity to schedule out my day. However I also know what I dislike about freelancing. I happen to like helping people, and being part of a team. So freelancing is not exactly the perfect fit for me, but it is still better than the last job I had.

Quit your job because you want better for yourself physically and mentally. Do not quit because you have not yet learned how to interact with others, because you don't like a certain aspect of your job, or because you do not like working for others. If we slow down and pay attention to our thoughts, we will notice cyclical patterns of negativity that can be changed.

Identify your own negativity patterns to overcome these hurdles. Personality conflicts will exist even after you quit your job. Even entrepreneurs have problems. With this being said, if a job is physically or emotionally toxic for you, go to human resources, or a manager you trust for help. That is the luxury of working for someone else. As an entrepreneur, you are human resources and you are responsible for resolving all conflicts.

If you are having trouble with a client, but you really need the money- guess what? You still have to work with that person until the job is done. Also, as an entrepreneur you will have to do a lot of extra tasks (sometimes for free) that you do not want to do. The same negativity triggers exist within you no matter what external environment you are in. I would argue that it is easier to resolve these conflicts in a full time setting, than it is as a freelancer- because you have less to lose financially, and more resources and support to help you succeed.

Many people will encourage you to quit your job if it doesn't make you happy. Here's a SECRET- There is no job in the world that will make you happy. Jobs are simply an transaction of time and services in exchange for money.

You have to make yourself happy, and bring that happy self to each moment of your day.

Some might think that quitting means you are unemployed, not making any income, that you are essentially on a stay-cation. Truth is, once I quit my job, I proved to myself that I could work harder than I had ever imagined. Freelancing is the hardest job I've ever had, and challenges me every day. It has positives and negatives, but overall I have proven to myself that I can survive as a freelancer. Whether or not it is what I want to do long-term, is another story. Here are some others who have succeeded after quitting their 9-to-5 jobs.

Barbara Saint Aimé is a professional publicist who was also a guest on my podcast. Barbara's glamorous job takes her all around the world, and even to the Golden Globes.

"I was there [at my 9-to-5] for six years and nothing was really happening for me, so I decided to look for another job, and it turned out that working for myself is the answer. I don't know if I'm rich but I do have a pretty amazing job."
-Barbara Saint Aimé, Publicist (Aimé Agency)

Alma Villegas-Schwalbenberg, PHD is a psychologist who runs a mental health practice.

"I was surprised at how my life ended up like this- being financially independent it's a gift. I never really imagined. I wasn't really pursuing wealth, I was pursuing helping people."
-Alma-Villegas Schwalbenberg, PHD

These entrepreneurs, my podcast guests and the survey participants mentioned in the next chapters have chosen to live the lifestyle that works best for them. I'm sure they would also tell you that they are not 100 percent happy all the time, and that there are parts of their job that they dislike. Certainly though, if you want to be an entrepreneur or freelancer, the benefits must outweigh the sacrifices. If you don't want to work at the job you hate anymore, there is hope on the other side. If you can master your mindset, and learn to understand your true motivations in life, you can make an informed decision that will not just provide temporary relief from stress.

The following chapters will provide resources so you can measure whether or not you should quit your job, and how to find the best career fit for you. Even if you decide to stay at your 9-to-5, there are creative tips for goal setting that can help you identify your ideal lifestyle.

In this book I will provide solutions that have worked for a variety of different people. Pick the solutions that work best for you and be open to experimentation. First, read on about the positives and negatives, and the reality of freelancing.

CHAPTER 4

MULTIPLE STREAMS OF INCOME EQUALS MULTIPLE SOURCES OF WORK

The popular theory about making money in today's economy is to have multiple streams of income. In other words, at least three ways that you make money. For example, as a video producer for a long time, the only income I had was from my full time (or part time) 9-to-5, creating videos. In 2012 I was working two jobs, one part time and one freelance. This was empowering because if I needed extra money, I could just pick up more hours at my freelance job. Or if the part time office was closed for a holiday, I could make time and a half at the freelance office. I now had two sources of income. After leaving the freelance gig, I started doing video productions of my own, as part of my production company. These were not steady assignments but I was now responsible for invoicing, finding clients, delivering the work- I was an entrepreneur, and this was my extra source of income outside of my day job.

When I started my podcast I expected that to be a possible way to make money, since a lot of podcasters out there pretend that they are getting rich from selling a free podcast download. To tell the truth, I have not made any money from my podcast, since it is a free program and I do it for the love of interviewing people and exploring this rich topic of creativity and money. However, it has been a way to promote products and services of mine which do make me some money. For example, I often promote my podcasting tutorial which teaches people how to make a high-quality podcast without buying expensive audio equipment (www.LauraMeoli.com/createapodcast). I am also writing this book because it is a life-goal of mine to be an author. Perhaps it will help me make some extra income. As a freelancer without that steady paycheck that I used to rely on, I receive income from at least five different sources per month. This is more difficult when it comes to filing my taxes of course, and more difficult when trying to calculate how much I make. However, I am succeeding at the multiple sources of income goal, because if one source goes away, I could potentially do more work in another area to make up for it. This model gives a lot of flexibility and you would not be relying on your relationship with one boss, in order to pay your rent.

Now some people who praise this model also try to make it sound easy. It is NOT easy to balance multiple sources of income. As I said, multiple streams equals multiple sources of work. I'd like to add to that and say it also means multiple sources of HARD work. Without a steady paycheck, the volatility of freelancing can bring a lot of anxiety and second-guessing. It is especially difficult in the months where I am not making as much as I used to make when I had a steady job.

The decision to leave a full time job as a main source of income is a scary one. Here is the reality of what it's like on the other side, as a freelancer, and some common misconceptions.

"I would recommend it [freelancing] to those who find themselves unable to fit into the traditional career molds. If you enjoy having some flexibility in when you work, what you work on and whether you want to pursue less lucrative passions outside of your career, then freelancing is for you. People should know their limits however and really consider whether this is the lifestyle they want."
-Anonymous survey participant
(Freelance TV/Film Editor)

"Freelancers can get a bad reputation as being lazy and just sitting around all day. I think this is because many people can't get their head wrapped around the fact that you don't have a boss or direct employer. The funny thing is that most freelancers that are successful, work harder than a captive employee. They are self-starters, hustlers, hard workers, driven, and often visionary. While we might answer to our 'boss' we do answer to our clients which can be a harder task."
-Michael Woodward: Freelance Web
Design/Development & Podcast Host

"Everyone thinks ANYONE can do this... all you need is to have the programs, but there is a lot of work, discipline and creativity that goes into this. Also, being a people person is key."
-Jamal Rolland: Freelance Video Editor

"People think I'm unemployed, or more accurately 'not working' which I find laughable. Yes, I get to work from home in my PJs with my cat sitting next to me, but I also never leave the office. I am always at work. I get

messages from clients about jobs or shoots at all hours, every day, with the expectation that I respond immediately."
—Diana Cherkas: Freelance Actor, Writer, Advertising Copywriter & Copy Editor

[The biggest misconception is] "That we are "helpers" to the Deaf community; that we donate our time and are not skilled professionals in our field."
—Jill Sniderhan, English/American Sign Language Interpreter

There is an assumption that if you like your work, you would do it for free. For someone whose job is helping others, I can relate to this frustration. No matter what field of work you are in, if you do it for free, you are undervaluing your own skills and negatively impacting your own industry. The phrase "passion project" really bothers me. I think a lot of people assume that if you are passionate about this work, then you cannot make it your full time job, or even a job that pays at all. Meanwhile, isn't that the ultimate dream? To make money doing what you love? If so, then we all need to stop asking people to work for free. If we are getting a grant or crowdfunding a project we are putting time and energy into, then we can't forget to pay ourselves. That is the only way we can justify taking time away from our paying "jobs." If we cannot pay ourselves for our time, how are we going to pay someone else for their hard work?

Since I graduated college, I have seen a huge shift in the technology required for filmmaking. Cameras that are on our phones do a great job of capturing clear and high quality footage that would have previously cost thousands or even millions of dollars to create in Hollywood. Everyone now thinks they are an expert at cinematography and filmmaking- so it has become very difficult to charge for video services. People just don't see the value. Plus, video is a hobby for most people now with social media, so it has fallen into a category of "fun" rather than "work" for hire.

> *"With the DSLR revolution, a lot of people picked up cameras and became cinematographers. Just because you can buy a camera doesn't make you anything. The other side of this is, it is really hard to be a full time filmmaker. It doesn't matter if you're a cinematographer or an art director or a writer or whatever. In Austria, the biggest film school, I went there once for an open house and the cinematographer teacher, he basically started his whole 'do you want to study here' thing with, '80% of the people in the film industry are unemployed'. It's probably not true in the States, but there are a lot of people aspiring to be creatives and there are very few people who continue to be creatives. What I'm trying to say is, be sure that is what you really want to do. You can try out things. If you want to pick up a camera, shoot a couple of things, and see if you like it. If other people respond to that and say, 'This is really great, I want to work with you again,' then maybe you can think about, 'Let's pursue this'. On a more practical note of things, to become a cinematographer is just go out and film stuff. Just keep doing things. Especially at the beginning, it's hard to get on projects. But just film and then edit, so you'll know what is working and what isn't."*
> *-Valentin Farkasch: Filmmaker & Photographer*

The best thing I would suggest to people in fields that are being phased out due to technology, is to pick up another skill. I am constantly taking classes and learning more to make me stand out in the job market. As a freelancer, I have time for this that I didn't always have when I was working full time. Being in charge of my schedule means that I can make education a priority, rather than limit myself to only learning the skills needed to execute the needs of my full time job. As a freelancer, if I am always learning new things, then I can truly have job security. Here are some of the best parts of freelancing.

"The freedom to work on your own terms."
–Michael Woodward: Freelance Web
Design/Development & Podcast Host

"Working on many different types of projects with many different types of clients. I've been at an agency who has a few main clients and you get a lot of work doing the same types of things. As a freelancer, I've been introduced to a wide type of work, with a wide variety of styles and workflows. As a freelancer, I've been able to pick and choose the best parts of work styles and workflows from each client and develop my own setup and style that suits me best."
–Bryant Coffey: Freelancer in
the Advertising Industry

"Being able to accept or turn down gigs according to my own needs. Some jobs are well paying, some are personally satisfying, some allow me to hone new and exciting skills. As a past example, I spent four months straight working only well paying jobs in order to put everything aside for six months and focus solely on producing a show. I put in more hours on the show, but theater doesn't pay nearly as well as advertising!"
–Diana Cherkas: Freelance Actor, Writer,
Advertising Copywriter & Copy Editor

Something to remember as a freelancer is that we do not have a steady or consistent paycheck. This can mean that we will make less money some weeks, than others with a full time job. It certainly is a trade-off for the lifestyle we want, but there are still bills to be paid. My strategy as a freelancer is that I have to charge more per hour, than my previous full time hourly rate. This is because I am not guaranteed to work eight hours a day, or forty hours a week, and not guaranteed that I will even have this same job next month. So depending on the assignment length, I have to price my hours accordingly to factor in the costs of running my business. There is overhead I have to consider, as an entrepreneur without a guaranteed income stream. The problem is that not every market location pays enough for that service. We are up against others who can do the job for less, and have to price our services in a sweet spot between what we can afford to live, and what clients are willing to pay us.

> *"The most difficult part of being a freelancer is working for myself. Therefore, if I don't close on a contract or happened to be sick for the day/week/month, I don't get paid. I also have to wear multiple hats (CEO, Marketing Agent, Accountant, etc.) in order to keep my business afloat. One day I will be able to hire professionals to do the job for me. Until then, I'm just fine wearing the many hats."*
> *-Alyscia Cunningham: Entrepreneur,*
> *Author, Filmmaker & Photographer*

> *"Working for yourself is more work. You're kind of everyone. You're the assistant picking up the phone. You're the boss sending emails, making decisions... you book your own travel. You're most of the time the accountant. You're everything, so it's a lot more work."*
> *-Barbara Saint Aimé, Publicist (Aimé Agency)*

"It's taken me a long time to get to where I'm at and I feel like it's just at the beginning. To deal with clients, stay current with trends, working long hours on short deadlines and cramming everything into 24 hours is a daunting task. You have to love the grind or else you won't make it out alive."
—Anonymous survey participant
(TV Editing side-hustler with a 9-to-5)

"Staying on track with your benefits, retirement plans and maintaining your savings account can be tenuous if you have a lot of breaks in between projects."
—Anonymous survey participant
(Freelance TV/Film Editor)

The main struggle is just that you can't really plan on any long-term basis. Most of my projects are maybe a month out, if I'm lucky. But a lot of calls are just like, 'Are you available tomorrow?' Planning anything or budgeting anything is a little nerve-racking."
—Valentin Farkasch: Filmmaker & Photographer

Sometimes I get excited about a project because of the creativity involved in it. Or I might get caught up in the negotiation phase and wanting to do whatever I can to be a part of that project. Of course projects that I like are going to be executed faster on my end, and so I can charge less for them. However, I do have to remind myself that this is a business, and my source of income. So I cannot always do people favors and work for a discounted rate. The most important thing that I have learned as a freelancer is that every moment is a potential for making money. This could be by meeting a potential client, or just knowing that the hours I am spending doing one thing could be used instead working on a paid project. As a freelancer I work a lot more hours, and execute a lot more assignments or jobs. The key is getting faster at what I do, without sacrificing quality. This way I can have more hours free for myself, or for another project. I am still getting used to it for sure, but it is definitely an important lesson to learn. There is no 9-to-5 paycheck anymore, so if I am not working, I am not getting paid.

> "It's easy to feel like you want to 'help' and in that process underbid a project. I think the key to the process is to properly assess the market, your value, and the amount of work available. You've got to pay your bills, so charge what is fair and treat your clients right. Don't bid the project based on fear: fear of rejection, losing the project, overbidding. Fear is never a good motivator. When I have taken projects on that were under the 'realistic' budget, I've always regretted. The client's response to your bid can be a great signifier of how the client will act when you are working on your project. Remember that not only do you have to be a good fit for them, they need to be a good fit for you too."
> –Michael Woodward: Freelance Web Design/Development & Podcast Host

> "I give my rate and if they think they can't afford me, I'm more than willing to negotiate if I really want the gig. What I find troubling are those creators who undervalue their work so much that they're willing to get paid $10 an hour and ruin it for the rest of us. I mean, if I'm going to shoot and edit your video for 10 dollars an hour, I might as well just be flipping burgers for the duration of the gig."
> –Alejandro Hernandez: Freelance Cinematographer & Editor

"Sometimes people come into an industry and say 'I don't really have capital, or connections. So I'm gonna lower my prices. I'm gonna provide cheap videography for people.' What that does is, you end up lowering prices in your field. You've pigeonholed yourself. You don't really make a profit and you end up getting clients that are not the type of clients you want. They're going to refer more clients to you that are also at that same price. You find yourself in a bubble."
–Lina Lansky, MBA: Filmmaker

You will see as a freelancer (if you decide to take the leap) that there is a lot of competition out there. Websites like Free-lancer.com, Fiverr, and Upwork have people competing from all around the world. There are also countless Facebook groups that post gigs multiple times per day. For those of us who live in more expensive markets like New York, Los Angeles, or San Francisco, we sometimes don't stand a chance at competing with freelancers with a lower cost of living.

When I started freelancing I was on these websites all the time. I spent hours looking for gigs and putting in bids, which are proposals or cover letters for a specific job. At times, the job postings would ask that you put in a lot of time and effort just to bid. For example, many video production jobs I applied to asked that I take a look at their current videos and suggest some ways they can improve. This is a fun creative exercise once or twice a week, but to make it a full time job is impossible. Think about it, to really do that question justice, I would have to spend about thirty minutes per bid. Out of about 100 bids that I put in that first month, I only got two jobs out of Upwork. Not all of them required a full analysis but a lot of them did, and with no hourly rate being made for bidding, I had to give up on this time-consuming process and look at where my time is better spent. I had the feeling that a lot of people asking for feedback in their bids were just looking for free advice from professionals, and not really serious about hiring anyone. Or that they were just going to go with the cheapest person they could find for the job, and use the feedback they liked as instructions. It really is a disappointing process and I do not plan on using it again.

> *"I don't bid jobs online. Period. Those sites like Upwork, Freelancer and whatnot are ridiculous in my mind. People are happy to work for peanuts and that's fine if they can get away with it, but then people expect me to do the same because they got it done with a cheaper person before. I've gotten very good at bidding jobs to clients in person and if I underbid, usually it's because revisions exceeded the budget, I let them know and generally it gets worked out. Usually, the best clients understand that our jobs are expensive to do and if they balk at the price, I know it's a potential red flag. That being said, if I overbid a job, I don't bill the client for the extra overhead I miscalculated. It comes in under budget, they're thrilled, and they call me back. Keep the clients happy and they will continue to call back."*
> *—Bryant Coffey: Freelancer in*
> *the Advertising Industry*

> *"I'm always more affordable than most, because I don't have constant overhead. As a casting director it is usually word of mouth or repeat clients. As a producer, I'm often asked to bid work that requires three bidders and it's usually awarded to someone they wanted anyway. It's a waste of time, but I'm getting faster and better at it."*
> *—Elaine Del Valle: Film & TV*
> *Director, Producer & Actress*

Every job has pluses and minuses. Something I dislike about freelance life is that I miss the social interaction of working with a team every day. While I do not miss the commute, it is counter-productive for me, to be in a quiet room alone all day. The social brainstorming and feedback is so important for my personality type. Luckily I have found some activities for myself that incorporate social interaction into my day, and into my creative process. One is my podcast. Making time to speak with someone on a deep level gives me an excuse to stop working and use my voice for a change. It is a great way to break up my week. Also, I make sure to incorporate a few lunch meetings to meet a friend, fellow freelancer or potential client. Getting out of the house is great, and I enjoy the opportunity to change up my routine. Another way to combat the loneliness of working from home is by attending networking events. This does double duty for me because it is a social interaction in itself, and then I have the opportunity to follow up with those I have connected with.

> *"I work the majority of my time from an office 10 feet from my house. I also have a co-working space at WeWork. Each have benefits and drawbacks. The key to working from home and not being isolated is to find a community in which you can engage regularly. This could be a weekly networking group, a creative group like Rising Tide Society, social groups, or even industry specific meetups. The key is that you need to be intentional and audit how you are doing. That self-awareness and purposeful plan can help to keep you from feeling alone. It takes work, but it's worth it."*
> *–Michael Woodward: Freelance Web Design/Development & Podcast Host*

"I still have to do a lot of networking. I understand this is the most important thing when I think about the fact that the best gigs I've ever had were thanks to references."
–Alejandro Hernandez: Freelance
Cinematographer & Editor

My best gigs have also been thanks to references from people I have worked with previously. The best situation for me is when someone is looking for a particular service that they are ready to pay for, and have found me through a reference. Referrals are very sporadic and unpredictable though. They come when they come, and there is no way to control them. I consider myself lucky when I get a high-paying client through a referral, because I'm not at the point yet where this work comes in consistently. I am learning to be patient and that things will happen when the time is right. Waiting for referrals requires a lot of faith, and constantly reaching out to my network.

"A lot of people think that when you become an entrepreneur you have so much free time on your hands. That your phone is ringing off the hook, that it's a fairytale, there are rainbows… My coach says that you need to dial for your dollars. You need to invite people to work with you.

It is such a humbling experience because in the back of my mind I'm thinking that I don't want to beg somebody that you need me. But when you start opening up and having that conversation, they will tell you that they need something and don't know how to get it. You have to show them how you can help. It's a really humbling experience when you have to go out there and find that next paycheck, that next client. Until you become this big time person where people are flocking to you, you're

going to have to flock to them. When you first step into the realm of entrepreneurship, people aren't beating down your door. You have to do a lot of leg work to be known."
     –Temica Gross: Budget Business Coach

"It's always good to be on the edge of your comfort zone. I think freelance is always going to be my role because you have to keep clients happy– keep selling, delivering and following up. There are three very different brains that you use for those. You have to be able to switch them on and off at any given time during the day. That's really awesome. [All the different roles we play] we never switch them all off. It's just that one has the mic more than the other. As a freelancer, don't ever switch off the salesman out of yourself inside. You always want to have the salesman there, watching for an opportunity, for the next client, being able to say to someone, 'hey, I might actually be able to help you with that'. Strike up a conversation and make that connection with with someone."
     –Brett Solomano: Hollywood Stuntman,
     Author, Speaker and Coach

Some people see networking events as a way to find new business leads. That is great for some, but a daunting task for others. My method of using networking events as a way to socialize really takes the pressure off of me. The key to freelancing is to make rules for yourself, and stick to them. For instance, I follow an honor system for which I only work with people who are trustworthy. Of course this does not apply to new clients as I don't know them yet. If someone proves to me that they do not keep their word, I usually believe them. Beggars can't be choosers, but I try to stick to this rule as much as possible. For example, a very uncomfortable part of freelancing for me, is having to follow up with people multiple times. It can become very discouraging when you are looking for work and don't have anything lined up. So what I do now is take the emotion out of it. If someone asks me to follow up, or agrees that I should follow up, then I do. I wait to hear a concrete confirmation of their interest, not just something polite disinterested people say like, "yes we should totally work together one day." There are just some people who don't like to say NO. It is easier for them to change the subject or give a brush off answer than to just be direct. Meanwhile, some people are just really busy or it might not be the best time to speak with me. It is my job to interpret their wishes and read the signals from them whether I should follow up again, or not. This is the single hardest part of freelancing, in my opinion.

> *"I have a pretty good sense about new clients and won't hesitate to turn down work if I feel it's a shady situation. I always use contracts, but taking someone to court would be devastating to me."*
> *—Bryant Coffey: Freelancer in the Advertising Industry*

A quick note about contracts. Always have a contract. Whether you have a company LLC or INC to protect your assets or not, it is best to have everything written out. This way, if there is any question or concern, you can always look at the contract. It is better to settle a dispute yourself than have you or your company's reputation dragged through the mud because of a disagreement. I've watched enough Judge Judy to know this for a fact.

The best client is the one that comes to me based off a referral. At times, yes, they are expecting to get a friend's discount. That goes back to my earlier note about not working for free- don't give discounts unless you can afford it. However, a referral means that I have a friend in common with this person, and they know my work already. I don't have to sell them on why they should work with me. Here are some other tips from freelancers who make and follow rules for their own success.

"There's definitely a lot of advice I could give to somebody who wants to freelance. The first thing to come to mind is building relationships and to create different resumes for different types of work. That's a really important one for trying to transition between narrative and reality [TV production] or to move up from assisting to editing, is have your assistant editor resume and then have your editor resume. There are career assistant editors. I really love assistant editing. I have a very important role on the pilot that I'm working on and any show I work on. Don't see it as a step back to assistant edit, to change career paths."
                    -Janis Vogel: Professional TV & Film Editor

"As a freelancer, you are often working on multiple projects for different clients at the same time. Having good systems for project management will help you turn the project around quicker and make your clients happier. It could be as simple as a checklist on a Moleskine notebook and a pen, or as complex and powerful web app like 17Hats. Finding what works for you and then using your system will make you more productive allowing you to grow your business or focus on other areas in which you define as success."
                    -Michael Woodward: Freelance Web
                    Design/Development & Podcast Host

"It's really tricky, in the beginning I would forget to eat. Literally I would wake up and my phone sleeps next to me on the nightstand so as soon as I'm up I'm on my phone,

and a lot of the business I'm doing is international so they're already up. So it's immediately I'm responding to emails as soon as I get up- not even a moment for myself. But then you kind of get up out of bed, and then right back at it. Oh crap it's 3:00pm and I haven't eaten anything all day. It's nonstop. It's finally now that I get up, I don't look at my phone until I'm ready to... I'm up, showered, find something to eat. I've just made that law for myself- I have to keep up with the regular world. I can't just be living in a cave where it's work nonstop. So the regular world gets showered and has breakfast and so that's what I have to do within my own home, minus the commute, which is great because I can work from my pajamas."
-Barbara Saint Aimé, Publicist (Aimé Agency)

"I would say, only if you have a safety net would I recommend freelance life to others. Don't just up and quit your job and hope for the best. I definitely got lucky to land a five-figure, one-month contract my first 8 weeks into it, but had I not, it would've been horrible. Make sure you're prepped and ready for the ebb and flow of this lifestyle, don't wing it."
-Bryant Coffey: Freelancer in
the Advertising Industry

A a common piece of advice I've heard from most people I've interviewed about freelancing and entrepreneurship is this: Don't get discouraged. It takes time to get a steady flow of work, and to get used to the lifestyle. I have worked ten years straight since graduating college (with a few short months off here and there in between jobs). Three months into freelancing, I wanted to go back to full time work. However, when I started looking at some of these full time jobs, I realize that it's not worth giving up the lifestyle I worked so hard to obtain. There is maybe the perfect full time job out there for me, but I haven't found it yet. I am getting closer to identifying that as I interview and stay open to possibilities. An important lesson I'm learning from the freelance lifestyle is patience and faith. Sometimes I'm not working every single day, and my anxious tendency is to start applying for work. Then there are these long periods where I don't have a day off for two or three weeks, and I'm rolling in cash (so to speak). With patience and faith I am learning to love my unpredictable lifestyle. Give yourself enough time to properly identify if something is right for you.

> *"I only teach [singing, piano and acting] for a living, I don't have any other job that sustains me. It took me one year to have enough students to pay my bills. It took 12 more years before I started creating online products and it's been 6 more years of trying to reach more people with my products. Which I am still in the process of figuring out and why I started working on the TV reality idea three years ago."*
> *-Julia Amisano: Singing, Piano & Acting Teacher*

I still am not sure how to identify my new lifestyle. It's a mix between freelance work, and entrepreneurship with some contracting mixed in. I don't like the term entrepreneur exclusively because we never truly work for ourselves. I always have a client or someone that I am reporting to. I've noticed, by identifying what I did not like about past jobs, that I am okay with having a boss, as long as I ultimately get to make some creative decisions. That choice alone is enough to shift from tedious, annoying projects to being excited about each new opportunity. We have to remember the balance of work and life. We have to know our own personality, what we enjoy, and make sure we are balanced outside of work, in order to stick with it. Otherwise we are just doing the same thing over and over, without learning from our mistakes.

I can see a very clear shift in the market for video production. People are just not paying as much for it anymore. It is up to me to be realistic and use my other skills and interests to grow my business. Otherwise I will be stuck in the past and always struggling.

> *"You have to be able to make your business what you want to commit to. And if you are a variety seeker, you have to find other things that will provide that variety seeker need so you can focus on your business. That is very tough to do. How do I get my variety seeker need, is it different hobbies? What I do on my off time so you have to find that out on yourself. The hardest part is finding out if your business idea is viable."*
> *–Alex Wood, co-founder of HoneLife*
> *and the Variety Seeker Tribe*

CHAPTER 5

SEMANTICS AND OPTIONS

A lot of people use the words entrepreneur, freelancer and contractor interchangeably for different purposes. Let me clarify and explain the different options you have.

A freelancer is someone who is not a full time employee for one employer. A freelancer might be a contractor or an entrepreneur, or both. A contractor is someone who works as an employee for a company on a freelance or temporary basis. They are usually paid per hour and get a W2 at the end of the year for tax purposes. Contractors and freelancers do not get health insurance or other benefits from one employer, as traditional full time employees do.

An entrepreneur can be a freelancer or contractor taking on projects and temp assignments from employers. The difference in being an entrepreneur (rather than a freelancer) is that you have a company. There is some kind of distinction that means when people hire YOU, they are hiring your company. You can facilitate transactions and provide services to individual people and not just work temp assignments for another company. When we think about entrepreneurship or owning a business in general, we see these acronyms: LLC, INC, and DBA. These are just legal distinctions that define a company's income structure for tax and legal purposes. You can have a company without filing for an LLC or INC- in which you would be doing business as (DBA) your company name. In this case, you are more at risk for liability or other claims of lawsuits against you because someone doing business as, can be sued for their own personal money. If you are LLC or INC, and get sued, the company gets sued, and has its money separate from those of the business owner. Someone might choose to be a DBA rather than LLC because yearly tax filing fees for LLCs and Corporations might be more expensive. So depending on how much income you make and business you pull in, it might not be worth it financially to spend the extra filing cost for LLC. If you get sued though as a DBA, you are in much more trouble because your personal bank account is at risk. I believe you can purchase liability insurance to protect your DBA in a similar fashion to LLC protection, however that is another fee where you have to weigh the potential risks and losses based on your income and work. If you want to be a sole proprietor doing business as your company name, you could easily obtain a Tax ID online for your business, even though you haven't registered your business with the state or formed an LLC/INC. It's all just logistics.

Now I am not a legal or tax expert, so I will not advise you on these matters. It would be wise to consult a lawyer and tax advisor to find out what is the best option for you.

An entrepreneur is responsible for the company, the invoices, paying taxes, purchasing items for the business, hiring employees, scheduling, branding, marketing and everything else that needs to be done to run a business. An entrepreneur usually finances all the expenses needed to keep their business going. You can view this as a burden, or a gift. With financial responsibility comes the power of making decisions. I love how Elaine Del Valle put it, when speaking about entrepreneurship as flipping the script to create opportunities for herself.

"I struggled my entire career. I was a financially successful

commercial actress. That's what I was- making more than what most legit actors make (day players or weekly players) because I make commercials. One day in residuals, you get so much money. I couldn't get hired legit to save my life until I wrote my play that showed them who I was and where I'm from. I couldn't get work at all, couldn't get anyone to look at me. Then things changed because I flipped the script. Now I make my own projects so even if I don't get a little part, that's okay because no one is going to write me a better part than I can write for myself. These are dream parts."
-Elaine Del Valle: Film & TV
Director, Producer & Actress

Being an entrepreneur is a huge responsibility and a personal decision. Both freelancing and entrepreneurship are riskier than working for a full time employer because you have to be responsible for your own health insurance, payroll and staffing. Getting payed is the riskiest part of freelancing. I have been lucky so far to have worked for trustworthy people, and have been payed for all the work I have done as a freelancer. However, there is no weekly or biweekly, or even monthly paycheck to rely on. Freelancers get payed randomly whenever they can. It is not uncommon to wait for more than a month, to receive payment for a job. So if you do not have any savings or a backup for how you are going to pay your bills, freelancing might not be a good choice for your just yet.

Entrepreneurship on the other hand, is something you could transition into. Maybe you could stay at your current job and build your business on the weekends, evenings and during your lunch break. There are a lot of entrepreneurs who wait to leave their full time job until their own business is successful enough to provide a steady income. It is really tough to balance, but potentially less risky than just quitting your job and hoping your business will do well immediately.

Remember that building a business takes time, just the way that making connections for freelance work takes time. If you can transition into it, that is the best scenario. The choice is ultimately yours.

"Entrepreneurship is one of the most important components in everything I do. Entertainment, real estate, even architecture- that taught me a lot about entrepreneurship. You have to be your own boss and be a master of your own hustle and just go hard."
-Teraj: Actor, Model and Musician

"When you get into it [starting your own business], or even if you haven't started yet but just thinking about it, whatever you believe to be true is not. I say that because if you're thinking it's going to be easy- it's not. If you think you're going to make an instant fortune in a month or even a year- you're not. Everything that you perceive it to be is untrue. However, you can do it if you're prepared to do the dirty work. Climbing the same personal ladder that you're climbing in corporate. You need that stamina and momentum to keep going. There are going to be more downs than ups in the first one to three years of entrepreneurship. If you are committed to whatever your vision is, whatever it is, you can definitely do it.

The problem I'm coming across is that people want that get-rich-quick scheme. Your one idea can probably be turned into three. Those three can be turned into a package or a bundle. [The mistake is] We're pushing this one idea hoping it'll spark interest, and maybe it does and then it fizzles out, or maybe it doesn't at all."
-Temica Gross: Budget Business Coach

"Entrepreneurship is not about that one, three point shot. It's about shots on goal. How many shots can you take? If you have one what you think is a great idea, then no. that's BS. Any good entrepreneur before they made it had behind them 8 or 9 trashed ideas that didn't work. That's the difference between winners and losers. The winners knew that it was about shots on goal and about potential good ideas."
-Alex Wood, co-founder of HoneLife
and the Variety Seeker Tribe

As a freelancer or contractor, who is NOT an entrepreneur with their own store-front business, you would generally have less responsibility, a more flexible schedule and usually get paid as an individual employee even though you are not a permanent staff member.

A freelancer can be an entrepreneur and a contractor. It is possible to just float around working different jobs as a temp, a contractor or freelancer, and not worry about hiring employees, branding, marketing, etc. You do not have to have your own company to be a freelancer, but you can if you want to. I choose to call myself an entrepreneur because it doesn't make sense for me to say I'm unemployed. I do work a number of temporary and part time jobs, and provide services to clients through my business. This is my choice because it works best for me at this point in time. So "entrepreneur" is the best way to describe myself, even though I do freelance assignments frequently as a contractor.

The definitions of an entrepreneur, contractor and freelancer will often overlap. Going forward, I will use freelancer to describe someone who does not work a traditional 9-to-5. You can interpret that as entrepreneur, contractor, or not. When it's time to decide if you want to be a freelancer, you'll choose the best definition for you. Just know that labels are fluid, and they don't usually matter. Most people will not investigate or do research to find out the details of your business structure. I'm not saying to be dishonest about it, just that this information is no one's business but that of you, your lawyer, your accountant and that of a potential employer.

> *"Being a freelancer is not for everyone and neither is a 9-to-5, and that's ok."*
> *-Alyscia Cunningham: Entrepreneur, Author, Filmmaker & Photographer*

There is another option for creatives who do not want to be a freelancer, but don't enjoy having a permanent full time job: Temping. There are temp agencies for every field and type of work. I recently worked a two-week assignment that paid very well, through a temp agency. It's not a job I would have applied to for full time work, because it does not have as much variety as I would like every day. However, for two weeks, it was great to make all that money and work with new people. I would definitely work for them again, but I am not obligated to. Being a temp means I have the power to decide.

If you are looking for a temp agency, it can be hard to find. I have applied to a lot of temp jobs in my career. The only time I got an actual response and meeting was after inquiring with a friend who does temp work in a different field. He made an email introduction that referred me to his temp agency who also has roles in my field, and that is how I am now affiliated with that agency. So the power of using your connections comes into play here even when looking for a temp assignment. If you are looking for work, be it a temp assignment, full time role or even new clients for your business, reach out to everyone you know. You might be surprised who responds with a good suggestion or connection.

The beauty of temping is that you are free to still do work on your own. You don't have to give up freelancing to take a temporary assignment. You can have your business, your freelance assignments, and keep your own projects going. If you want to make some steady income for a short amount of time to offset the instability of freelancing, a temp assignment is an option to consider.

Whichever of these freelance paths you decide to take (if any), don't let labels stop or delay your progress. I spent a lot of time (and money) trademarking my business name, researching business incorporation, registration and SEO strategy because that is what other people said I should do. Truth is you have to do whatever works for you. There are no set rules on how to start your business, or become a freelancer. There is only advice. Just because you trademark your company name, register or incorporate your business, or create an expensive website doesn't mean you will magically get clients banging down your door. Even though I have a business website, put up a few social media ads, and created flyers, I received most of my freelance jobs from word of mouth and by reaching out to people directly. It has been helpful to have a tax ID for security purposes but it was not necessary for me to purchase liability insurance or become an LLC. Having done that would have been a lot of extra money and time taken away from working on projects.

I encourage you to visit SCORE.org, FreelancersUnion.org and/or your local small business association to find out more about running your own business. Remember that these websites are offering advice, not rules. You have to do what works best for you and do what will make you money- not what other people say are the necessary steps, to obtain what they have.

Being a freelancer is just as hard as working full time, except you are interviewing for jobs and selling yourself much more often. Focus on your communication skills, pitching, and gaining as much knowledge and skills as you can. It doesn't matter what you call yourself as long as you are offering value to your clients and paying the bills.

CHAPTER 6

WORKING FOR YOURSELF?

Later in this book, I will uncover my special formula for finding and combining your multiple skill sets to create your ideal career. First, it is important to understand that other people don't care what your multiple skill sets are. Honestly, everyone is self-interested. Clients are coming to you for a product or services because they need something specific that you can offer. They are not paying you to combine your passions, challenge yourself creatively and grow as an artist. I'm sorry if you're just hearing this for the first time. Don't kill the messenger.

I mentioned it briefly in the freelancing chapter, but it's worth expanding upon. When we quit our 9-to-5, we do not quit working for others. Unless you are very wealthy and have no bills to pay, our business model as a freelancer will be to work for others creating things that they need. For example, as a freelance filmmaker, I am hired as a videographer to shoot local events. While I do have the choice in which assignments I say yes to, if I need the money that month, I will likely shoot anything that pays the bills. My skill is videography in this case, and I am being hired to execute the vision and task put before me by an employer. That employer can be a local TV station, a small business owner, or a non-profit organization. My specialty here is videographer.

Another role I typically play is that of marketing video producer and editor, where I work with business owners to conceptualize and execute a video, graphic design or podcast to help them achieve their goals. This role has much more responsibility than if I were to be hired as a videographer who is just dropping off an SD card with recorded video and not delivering the end product. As a business owner, I have to make sure the clients who I create these videos for are happy in the end, and throughout the process. It is much more creative, but definitely requires more follow-through. My specialty here is as a full-service production company. Anything the client needs, I can execute, and I have business associates to fill in the gaps of things I need help with or want to outsource.

In both cases, I am certainly working for someone else. Even though as a production company, I do have much more creative input, because the client is paying the bill, and THEY are in charge of the end product. The client has the need and I provide a service. It is important we remember this when we quit our 9-to-5. If we want to make money, there will always be a boss who needs us to do something. Unless we are financing our own project, we will always be working for someone else.

In fact, as a freelancer you will have many more bosses than you would as a full time employee. Even if you have a huge bureaucracy of people higher in the chain of command at your 9-to-5, you typically only report to one or two people. As a freelancer, each client that wants a product created is my boss. Every TV station that I work for has a boss or two, and even my temp assignments have bosses. If you don't like answering to people, quitting your 9-to-5 does not solve that problem. Luckily, I enjoy working with people and collaborating, so this is not an issue for me.

The transition to freelancer can be tough, but the best advice I have heard thus far is from one of my clients. He said that he only works with people who are pleasant to work with. If they prove to not be trustworthy, or a pain in the butt, he does not work with them. If he needs the money and doesn't have much of a choice in who he works with that month, he might charge that pain in the butt client more. You have to value your time, have integrity, know what you have to offer and to whom. Relationship building is key. If you find people you enjoy working with, and vice versa, they will refer you, and your network will grow to include other quality clients. Be careful of the company you keep when it comes to clients. Sometimes we need to just take any job possible to pay some bills, but if we have prepared for the jump to freelance by saving up, we can start off on the right foot.

> *"Know who your target audience is, and who your ideal customers are. So, you're gonna have to do a little bit of market research to know where you're going to actually position your program, your product or your service. You're not going to advertise a weight loss supplement in a daycare. You want to make sure you're targeting the right people."*
> *-Temica Gross: Budget Business Coach*

> *"It is really tough and there is no doubt about it that it is just hard to transition between fields or transitioning from being an assistant to being an editor. It's always that first time. For editors, every project I've had I've said, 'this is my first action-based documentary series reality show, or this is my first pregnancy-related documentary series show. This is my first short narrative film'. It's always a first because every project is so unique. I wouldn't have been able to transition from reality television to fiction without the help of my friends. You have to build relation-ships and those relationships have to be organic to you."*
> *-Janis Vogel: Professional TV & Film Editor*

"It's a relationship game. For the most part it's building relationships, and it's cultivating that relationship after you've built it. And it's not necessarily that I'm connecting with you, and as long as you've connected that's the end of it. NO. I'm going to connect with you, I'm gonna keep communicating with you, I'm gonna be in the places where you will be. I'm on social media all the time liking her posts. [I'm going to the event she attends and introducing myself, setting up a call] but then once you make the connection I can't just stop liking her tweets. So this is me cultivating the relationship.

We need to be cultivating these relationships so that eventually my idea seems like it's their idea... Now as I'm cultivating relationships, I'm getting in so many development executives' ear. I didn't go through the typical way that everybody went through. I said, 'hey I need your advice for my book' that was one way I got through the door."
—Squeaky Moore, Author of "100 Pitches,
Mistakes I've made so you don't have to"

"Never be afraid to speak up, whether it's speaking your mind or if you see someone that is an idol of some sort. Don't be afraid to walk up to that person and strike up a conversation. Just speak up because you'd be surprised that by simply opening your mouth, how many opportunities can come about that way."
—Teraj: Actor, Model and Musician

Often times we will have to reach out to strangers and pitch ourselves in order to get hired and find a new client. This can be exhausting and provide few results if you are just starting out as a freelancer.

Like Squeaky, I used a non-traditional means to reach out to people. My podcast has helped me connect with people I otherwise would have never spoken to. These are authors, musicians, friends of friends, etc. Once I had a reason to reach out that was relevant and beneficial to them, they had a reason to respond. I got a better response rate than just sending a cold-email asking for a job. Use your connections and think creatively about how you can catch an employer's eye, whether it be a full time or freelance opportunity.

CHAPTER 7

FINDING YOUR WHY

When I graduated college, I made a list of my ten-year goals. On that list was to find work as a creative video producer. That goal was my most basic and safe one, as most people who graduate from college hope to find a job doing something related to their studies. Further down the list was the goal of teaching video, film or TV in college. At the time, I left the list pretty general, just writing the word TEACHING on there, but I knew inside that I wanted to become a professor. With no job lined up, nothing to occupy my time, and student loan debt to pay back at some point, I was like most people are when they graduate- hopeful and lost. Let's identify where my goal of teaching came from so I can explain why making a very general ten-year list of goals is not a good idea for most people.

As a sophomore in college, I started working a paid internship position as a producer and editor creating news pieces and corporate marketing videos for a show called Transit Transit News. The news director was Winston Mitchell, who quickly became my mentor. I was given the opportunity to work with some other very important people in my life who made a huge impact on my career, like Amanda Perez. She was my TV writing teacher in college, who helped me get the Transit News job which changed my life. For the first time, I had proof that I could receive a paycheck for creating videos. This was powerful proof not only for my parents who probably were worried about me going to film school, but also proof for me. When I decided to transfer out of my journalism program and go to film school, I had flashes of the same values that I have now as a freelancer. I knew that I am not the type of person who wants to just work nonstop doing something I don't love. I wanted a career, and even though being a video, film or TV producer is risky and competitive, it's something I had so much curiosity about. I couldn't NOT go to film school. Just a year or so after following this curiosity, I found myself getting paid to make videos. This is why I believe so much in following your curiosity. If you want to do something, try it. The universe, or God, or whatever you believe controls all of this that's going on, will give you a sign that you are on the right path. This first paycheck was my sign.

Back to my goal of teaching. Amanda who helped me get the job at Transit News also sparked my interest in teaching. She showed me that as a teacher, I could be not just someone who gives lectures, but someone who is there for my students when they need me. She showed me that being a teacher was not just about giving grades, but about giving advice and guidance. Winston's internship program at Transit News was also giving me signs that teaching might be a good path for me. It was a very hands-on training program where the senior interns trained the new interns on all aspects of video production. This program was instrumental in giving the news anchors, hosts, videographers, editors and producers who work today on national and local news stations across the country, their very first opportunity. I was lucky enough to go from junior to senior producer pretty quickly, and I was given the chance to teach interns all aspects of video production. I loved it.

Amanda and Winston helped me discover my love for teaching and training, which became a long-term goal of mine. At the time, college professorship was less competitive, and I was under the impression that with 10 years of experience in the field, I could become a professor without a master's degree. So, believing that was a possibility, I threw myself into my work, not worrying about grad school.

Ten years later, the requirements for professorship have changed dramatically. Most colleges now require a PhD in order to teach, not just a MFA or MA. I believe this is because of how competitive the field has become. Also, because a lot of film schools are looking for famous professors to add to their staff list, as a way to attract more students to their program. The increased requirements for professorship have not stopped me from achieving my goal of teaching. Just like no requirements or rules should stop YOU from achieving your goals. Here's how I did it.

In 2011, I started working for a college as a video producer and editor. This was after learning the recurring lesson of not forcing myself into a job that isn't right for me (more on this in a later chapter). This Higher Ed job was a good fit for me but lacked a few things. Since my previous jobs were so much more fast paced and time consuming, I had a lot more free time on my hands, and I had no idea how to spend it. I realized that I could use this free time to grow my skills outside of work, by pursuing my other passions and following my curiosity.

Even though it was two years since I had graduated from the Transit News job where I was a teacher, I still was teaching quite frequently, in different ways. At each job I had worked, I was being asked to train new employees and interns. My friends and colleagues were always asking me for input on their own creative projects. No matter what job I was working, I was somehow teaching someone something. I just didn't know how to turn that hobby into a paid job skill.

"The people that are receiving your talent and your gift for free, that's the confirmation you need to know that you can indeed sell it. The people that are going to pay for your services are not going to be the people that were able

to reap the benefit of the free service before- and that's okay. That's fine. You only needed to know that what you're doing is accurate and it actually works because people want it. They just simply don't want to pay for it but they know and believe in your talent so much that they continue to come back to you asking for this service.

When you go out now and step into the world to sell it, you have that confidence in knowing this thing, whatever it is, is a need for someone out there because I have 30, 40 or 50 testimonies behind me that says so. Even if they received it for free. People that are going to buy your product or service are not going to be your best friend, or your cousins, it's going to be someone who actually needs it. It's often said that the people who support us most are not our friends and family, and this is true. But you shouldn't become offended by that. Simply take their support in the past as confirmation that what you're doing is right."
-Temica Gross: Budget Business Coach

First, I started tutoring on a website called WyzAnt, and was able to do one on one teaching in my field. Usually, these assignments were close to home, and I set my own hourly rate. Here I was finding a way to teach, even if it's not in the form I had imagined. However, I was not doing enough of these tutoring gigs to leave my university job, and it was not something I wanted to do all the time because of the odd hours.

Months after I started tutoring for Wyzant as a side-gig to my full time job, I had a job interview with a local film organization that has an education program in our local community. I wanted to know more about this non-profit that I never heard of before, so I got my foot in the door by applying to a job that quite frankly I was not qualified for. The meeting proved to be very beneficial in that I was able to meet like-minded people with a similar mission. We have to remember that no matter who we are meeting and for what purpose, that we have to best represent ourselves and our own personal mission. That could mean having multiple resumes for multiple specializations, or just telling the appropriate story during an interview so a potential client can understand your wealth of experience in that particular area. We have to realize what our value is and what we can bring to others, even if they don't realize they need it yet. Keep an open mind, an open heart, and don't be afraid to specialize in multiple areas.

"Value was another spiritual journey that I went on. Learning how to value myself and value my work. Why are these things important? Because you cannot go into a pitch meeting and not value yourself or your work and win. You can't win in a pitch meeting if you go in with the mentality of, 'Is it good?' I had to get ahold of that. My 100 Pitches journey was about getting ahold of my faith and me valuing myself and the quality of my work.

I didn't even get on this podcast today without doing the necessary work to build up my confidence in myself, to appreciate myself before I could get in this call to talk about what I'm talking about. I had to develop a morning routine to be able to reach out to people to say, 'I need to have a call'. That needs a certain amount of gumption, a certain amount of balls to be able to get on there.

Otherwise, when I get on, I sound wimpy and unsure of myself. I write about the moment, it's not about the spiritual side, but just the moment when I realized [this was]... yet another pitch. Pitching to try to break the pro-verbial wall of getting through the door or break the door

down or whatever, to get through the gatekeeper is a pitch."
—Squeaky Moore, Author of "100 Pitches,
Mistakes I've made so you don't have to"

"When you walk into an audition, even if you don't get the part, represent who you are and what you have to lend to the next part. You have to be on that casting director's mind when the next part comes in... So, it's all what you're the most right for. Even if you're an actor and you walk in for a co-star part (under 5 lines), if you get that part, it doesn't matter how many lines it is. Do you know how hard it is to get that part?"
—Elaine Del Valle: Actress, Writer,
Producer & Casting Director

Even though I did not get the job I applied for, I later became a teacher for the Pelham Picture House. Again, this is not the form of teaching I had imagined when I put it on my list of goals, but the timing was right. My university job was lacking in the teaching and creative aspects that I craved, and I considered enrolling in grad school to become an art teacher for high school or college students. I wanted to learn more about education but getting an MFA in film or video just didn't feel right for me since I was already starting to feel the physical strain of all the years spent lifting heavy equipment. I also didn't feel like I wanted to spend the money for a graduate degree in something I already had so much experience in. Teaching was the curiosity that I wanted to follow, not production.

My teaching gig at the Pelham Picture House started as an opportunity to teach documentary film to a group of 5th grade girls at the Boys and Girls club. I worked out my schedule at the university job so I could do this on my days off. The first two or three sessions were so nerve-wracking and exhausting. I had no idea how to teach kids, and I was reaching out to all my teacher friends for advice. It was the education director at the Picture House, Francile, who was my biggest cheerleader. She helped me through the everyday struggles and still to this day leaves me in awe when it comes to her ability to understand kids and relate to them. The documentary film class became a lot easier once I took away my expectations that these kids were going to behave the way interns used to behave at Transit News. These kids were taking this class for fun, not to get a career in video production. The documentary was about this Boys & Girls club raising money to buy filters for Flint Michigan after their water crisis. Only after I took away my expectations of how they should behave, did this become the perfect job for me. The kids and I were able to connect to this project on a deeper level, and in turn connect to each other.

> *"Over the years, I've had so many side hustle jobs when I was in the music industry. One of them was a paralegal. I used to have to go to all these networking conferences. BNI, the Business Networking International, they always talked about givers gain. I always thought that was such an interesting way to frame it. I've just learned over the years that it's not only just putting good karma out there, it's not just like, 'be a better person and help others'. That's what we want to come out of it. It's also just shifting your mindset because when you get so involved in your own work and how it's going to help you and what you're going to get out of it. It really just makes it tunnel vision and you're not seeing the bigger picture. When you get out of your own head to help somebody else, you're actually opening yourself up to see what more is out there. It's really like a mindset exercise more than anything."*
> *-Suzanne Paulinski: Mindset Coach for Musicians & Industry Professionals*

That experience teaching while also creating a video to raise awareness for an important issue- helped me understand WHY I love teaching media production. It's not important that I started out by wanting to teach in college. The age of the students is just a detail. By connecting to the reason WHY this was a goal rather than the specifics of WHAT the goal looks like, I now understand myself on a deeper level. Now, I can take on, or turn down assignments based on my own personal goals. Again, the universe, or God, or whatever you believe in, has shown me that I am going in the right direction. Even after leaving my university job, I continue to work for this organization. I have been teaching at the Picture House for more than two years, and enjoy the new challenges that come with new age groups, new classes and subjects. I love teaching because it allows me to help young people see the possibilities for their future by honing their creative skills. My art and music classes were so important for me as a teenager. I want to give my students a creative outlet, and teach them communication and creative skills that they can apply to their work and life. Here are some other freelancers who have identified the reason WHY they do what they do.

"My fundraiser is for foster kids. I was a foster kid growing up, and I wanted to be able to give them a voice. Especially for all the foster kids that have dreams, when they get older that they feel like nothing can be accomplished. They're so young and have so much of this world to accomplish those things once they get out of foster care. Then again, they don't have parents to help them with finances once they get out.

A lot of them become homeless. Some of them while in the foster system get mistreated. There are so many kids in foster care and a limited amount of people. I wanted to start a fundraiser for a bunch of foster kids to raise their voice. It will be based on their dreams. Take photo shoots of them

create their dream for a day. Those images will go into a gallery. All proceeds will go towards the kids when they age out of foster care, that they will have money to help them."
-Michelle Engberg: Professional Photographer

"I'm driven by presenting female or Latino driven truths.... So, work with good people, and do what you say, mean what you say, and represent."
-Elaine Del Valle: Film & TV Director, Producer & Actress

"I jumped into the realm of entrepreneurship and into wanting to be a budget business coach because I knew I was going to start a business. I didn't know exactly what I wanted to do until I realized what my niche really was. That was motivating and encouraging other people to do the same thing. Not just all other people- it was more so mothers, single moms or fresh out of college entrepreneurs. I even had some clients who were in their upper sixties. They were ready to start their business even that late in the game. Everyone had shared the same pain point and that was 'I don't have the money'. Money should NOT be the reason why you don't start your business. There are many many people in this country who have no money but they have the vision. All you need is the vision."
-Temica Gross: Budget Business Coach

"Really, that's the whole theme of the book [The Rock/Star Life Planner]. That's the whole theme of my company, is when you want that confidence and you feel shaky or you

feel like you're not deserving of where you are or where you want to go, the first step is to write out WHY. Why is it going to be the most important thing? Why are you doing what you're doing? Why do you feel that you don't deserve this? Why do you feel like people are going to say these things or have this reaction to you that maybe you don't want them to have? Getting back to that whole WHY thing is really, really important because it directs us in everything that we do. Sometimes all it takes is getting back to the why you're doing what you're doing. When you know your why, sometimes that breeds enough confidence in us to keep going."
—Suzanne Paulinski: Mindset Coach for Musicians & Industry Professionals

It can be difficult to remember how we got to this place of work, work, work. When we are so often meeting new people, we eventually get good at molding our specialization to meet their needs. This sometimes leads us to forget the ultimate big picture. Especially if we like to help people, it becomes so easy to forget what we want personally, and we get caught up in the motions rather than the intentions behind them.

"The way to get opportunities is to genuinely value the relationships that you have and to build on new ones. Not in a self-serving way. With a lot of great artists, the approach is 'listen to me, listen to this' whereas I think the approach of 'what can my music do?' and 'who can I serve?' That is essentially a much more effective approach— when it's done genuinely. I like to think and I hope that we're making a positive change in this world. That's really my goal."
—Alex Bondarev: Refugee & Indie Singer- Songwriter from The Bronx

*"What are you good at? What are your talents? Using
your talents what is the best way to serve humanity?"
-Alex Wood, co-founder of HoneLife
and the Variety Seeker Tribe*

Everything you do should contribute to your bigger picture. If part of that bigger picture is helping others achieve their goals, or serving a greater purpose, make sure you have not become too self-interested. That might mean taking on a non-paying gig, or working for less than your normal rate. Remember why you signed up for this, and enjoy the benefits of helping others. Some of the most rewarding projects I've worked on have been the least financially lucrative. It's up to you to measure the value of every opportunity, and trust that your intentions will get you to where you need to be in your career.

Take a step back from the everyday tasks and give yourself time to connect to your WHY. There are many possibilities for why we want to achieve certain things. Your WHY might be to financially support and/or inspire your children, family or spouse. Other WHYs could be more specific. For example, we might want to have a certain amount of money saved so we could have a down payment towards the house we want to purchase. As part of Brett Solomano's 28 day Momentum Mastery course, we were challenged to keep digging deeper. This was a huge help for me, to ask for the WHYs beneath the WHYs. You can always go one level deeper. If you want to save money for your house, why do you need a house? What will owning a home change about your lifestyle? Can you achieve that same goal in some other way? This line of questioning helps us think outside the box we've put ourselves into (when we set goals).

Another challenge when you write down your WHYs, is to look for which of those are ego-driven. Do we want a house because it will impress someone? Don't make your WHYs about anyone else's perception of you, because perception is speculative. We don't actually know what other people think about us, and even if we did, why should we care? Make your opinion of yourself the most important, and let your opinion be based solely on how well you live up to your own values. That means, what is something we can BE (not achieve, not buy, not have), and how can we BE that, as often as possible? Some examples of values could be generosity, or kindness, or honesty. My meditation lessons with the Brahma Kumaris World Spiritual Organization have helped me define myself as a being of creativity, honesty and love- not as a video producer, an employee or a freelancer.

We could always improve, that's the beauty of life. Don't get caught up in measuring your failures or all the times you were not living up to your values. Make goals and define your WHY as a daily challenge that you can achieve in each moment, not a goal that is measured by outside judges or credentials. Yes, we could certainly have goals like winning an award, or obtaining a higher degree of education. However, I challenge you to dig deeper into that goal setting process. Why do you want to get that degree? For me, I want to obtain my Master's and eventually my PhD because I want to explore my curiosity, I want to learn, and I want to know as much as I can so I can teach others.

My other example, why do you want to win a certain award? I have been entering my videos into the NY Emmy Awards for years. When I was finally nominated, I felt on top of the world. Got all dressed up, went to the ceremony and lost. Yes, it is certainly an honor just to be nominated, but I was looking at it all wrong. I wanted this award so I could feel better about myself and my efforts. This was after all, the same time I was working for the university job that left me feeling very creatively stifled. I was nominated again the year after, went to the ceremony again and lost again. Same thing. On the third year I was nominated, but decided not to go to the ceremony. I don't think I could have got my hopes up for the third time, and be let down. My ego couldn't take that. So instead,

I planned a small gathering of friends at home which happened to be on the same evening. We had a great time and I honestly am glad I didn't go to the ceremony that year, even though that was the year I WON.

After countless years of wanting to be nominated, two more years of wanting to actually win, and I finally had achieved this goal of winning an Emmy award that was on my ill-conceived list. The most surprising thing about winning was that it didn't change anything! I still felt stifled, unhappy, and unsure when it came to my career. The achievement didn't change how I felt inside. It wasn't until I started defining myself by my values rather than my roles, that I found some clarity. It was a long process for me, but my curiosity and introspection helped a great deal. Why did winning an Emmy award not change anything? - because awards don't measure who we are internally. They are subjective physical representations of achievement bestowed upon us by other people, comparing us to our peers.

While it is great to know that others see how much hard work I put into my videos, it didn't make me want to work any harder. In fact, it made me want to work less because I realized that my goal was not all I expected it to be. There is no connection between winning an award and being happy. So, when you are writing your WHYs, really think about who you want to BE. Write WHYs based on your values, not based on external circumstances. If you do this, you will reach your goals each day rather than chasing them forever.

"There's only so much you can do in one day as far as baby steps towards your goals. Update it every year and you write it down in paper... the old school way. But whatever, do it on the phone, write it down, get it out of your head. You see what we're doing? We're pulling it out of our sub-conscious. You're clearing a space in your brain. You've got to do that. Five-year plan, it just gives you this overarch-

ing daily confidence, because you will see that when you delete a lot of the fluff in your day that clogs up your mind about self defeat and why you can't and rejection. I told you, I got dropped by a modeling agency today. It was a three-year modeling agency contract and I've never been happier because it's a new door and I'm going to kick it down and smile and introduce myself. That five-year plan is this overarching sense of confidence throughout you every day because you know where you're going, you have very clear picture of the life that you're building brick by brick."

-Jacob Bacaner: Entrepreneur,
Fitness Model & Coach

"Maybe some of those goals on your five-year plan aren't really for you anymore. I think we make these five-year goals or annual goals or whatever they may be and we change and we learn and we grow and other things take our attention away. We don't stop to think: 'Did I get distracted or did I stop getting passionate about what I was on?' We're either avoiding something out of fear or we're avoiding something because we no longer care about it. We have to always, whether it's weekly or monthly, take that time to reflect on those things. That is part of self-care. Taking the time to be like, 'I'm going to walk away from this and go see my friends and recharge' because when we socialize with the people we care about, we're [truly] ourselves."

-Suzanne Paulinski: Mindset Coach for
Musicians & Industry Professionals

I like to write down my WHYs and the lessons I learn from the journey, as often I can. That is part of the reason I am writing this book, to have a record of why I am where I am. Take at least fifteen minutes to write down these WHYs today, and then go back to that list and question all of them until you have a specific and refined list. Then, set a calendar reminder one year from now, so you can reassess your value-based WHYs.

You can update your list before then, but make it a point to update your list especially when you come to a new realization or set a new big-picture goal for yourself (coming up in a later chapter). If you're not into list-making, you could try creating a vision board, or write on your mirror, or draw something… whatever works for you. Put the 'list' somewhere visible, where you won't lose it or forget it. Make it impossible to forget your WHY.

CHAPTER 8

GOAL-SETTING

I first created a goals list for myself as a piece of advice I heard from a friend who was killing it, hitting every goal on their list. He even had his list framed and in a prominent place in his home. When I did this assignment for myself, that framed list of goals became a daily reminder of my failures. It gave me anxiety and made me worry that I could never achieve all of these things. It made me feel bad about every day because if I wasn't doing something towards one of those goals, then what was I really doing?

My anxiety snowballed and I began wondering if I would ever achieve ANY of my goals. For the sake of my own sanity, I threw the list in the garbage. For some, having a clear vision of their future goal and a timeline laid out, is a great motivator. But for me, it just doesn't work. I need to be in the moment and have gratitude for each day, whether or not it leads me to this list of tasks to accomplish. Life is filled with expectations that we will live the status quo, or get a regular job, and all the things that people tell us we should do. When something isn't working for you, change it. That could mean becoming a freelancer, or moving to another country, or something as small as changing the goals-list exercise.

At this time, I do have a list of goals I'd like to accomplish, but I do not have it printed. Actually, it's buried somewhere in my files folder on my computer and not too easy to find. What I did to that list to make it work for me, is write out all the things I had accomplished so far in one column. This starts out the assignment from a place of gratitude, not a place where we feel inferior. Next, I wrote out only those really big goals that I want to accomplish. No details, no timetable or expectations that I will know HOW I'm going to accomplish that. This was inspired by my learning why teaching is a goal, but not necessarily knowing how it would manifest, or in what form. Keeping my WHY in mind, it was easy to make this list. Here are some of the goals on my list- *Create and host my own podcast, travel abroad, own property, and write a book.*

Buying property is on there because at the time I was renting and moving around a lot. I wanted to know that I had a stable place to live so that I could feel comfortable exploring the next phases in my career and my life- without worry that I will have to move again. It is for stability and peace of mind so I can be my best and most relaxed self. The other goals on that list are all tied to teaching. Travel abroad so I can gain a bigger perspective on the world, and share those experiences through my podcast and book. By leaving these goals very vague and without a timeframe, I am letting the universe take care of the details. If you don't believe in the universe, or God, you could think of it as getting the stress of that off your mind. You're only hoping for the end destination, not to micromanage the path to get there.

Here are some other goals that made that same list- *Be kind. Be creative. Be open.* These are reminders of how I want to BE in each moment, and they are value-based. I'll just be surprised and grateful for each achievement as it comes along, rather than worried about setting them in motion. Life is much better with surprises.

Also on my re-imagined goals list are a few things to try, or a list of possibilities, rather than goals. Possibilities give me the flexibility to try something new and analyze how I feel about it. Not just to say that I must do this thing, and assume that it will be everything I want it to be. This leaves me open to receive unexpected blessings and opportunities. Just because I haven't planned something doesn't mean I can't enjoy it. For example, a recent music video I directed was planned out carefully. When on set, I discovered a fog machine was available. I couldn't turn down the opportunity to add something so special and fun. The band even told me that this was their favorite part of the final video. It is spontaneous things like that, the universe sends as a way to enjoy life. Be playful and embrace the moment.

For most very successful people, a list of goals may be appropriate, but for me, I'd rather embrace the moment and be happily surprised when big things happen. This is how I manage my anxiety and keep feelings of failure at bay. Do what works for you. While we are setting these goals for ourselves, it is important to measure our past and present.

> *"To achieve the best self is a constant look inward at the self and a constant passion of learning more about ourselves, the negative as well as the positive. And also exploring parts of the self in relation to the environment, we are open to new learnings, new people but also take care of the people we associate with. So, the highest self is within but we have to listen. We cannot achieve the highest self if we are worried about the future, and also don't be influenced by your own notions of ourself even if we have the habit of putting down ourselves. All these tendencies we have to stop listening and believing these thoughts that come to our mind."*
> *-Alma-Villegas Schwalbenberg, PHD*

I believe that life is cyclical; we go through ups and downs naturally. I used to think about this as a bad thing, where if I'm having a good day, I used to anticipate that it wouldn't be much longer until things go bad again. Certainly, my mindset has changed quite a bit since then. There is good and bad in every day of our life. Every moment, in fact, can be both simultaneously good for one person, but heartbreaking for another. Rather than looking at our life in this black and white, we should work with a formula for what feelings truly are:

$$Action \times Perspective = Feelings$$

Feelings can be seen as a momentary, fleeting emotion. In this instance, we should use this formula to think of our feelings as a big picture. Are we happy with where we are in this moment of our life? Are we happy with the momentum we are making towards our goals? So, not happiness in the sense of temporary joy and excitement, but a lasting, big picture contentment. Not emotional reactions but an overall sense of satisfaction. Specifically, are you okay with where you are in your career and where that career is potentially going? What about your life? If not, it's time to make a change. Actions can also be thought of as your situation, or your effort towards a goal. It is whatever is going on in your life at the moment, externally. I choose the multiplication symbol because your perspective can blow any little instance way out of proportion. The better your perspective, the better your feelings will be, no matter what actions are occuring. So when doing the following, keep your perspective in mind for each instance. Were you in a good mindset or a bad one? Try to have a positive perspective when going through this next chapter so you can focus on the growth you gained from each experience.

Here's the assignment which I have heard so many times, combined and tweaked a bit based on my research and personal experience. Get a piece of paper, or open up a new word document on your computer. Let's create your Past Career Assessment.

First, take a huge sheet of paper and make a line going down the middle from top to bottom. Or if you are working on this digitally, create a table with two columns on a word document.

Next, make rows with lots of space underneath, for each job you've ever had. This could be a paid job, an internship, or an experience you've had that is important to you. You could definitely do one job at a time to get the appropriate spacing correct, but if you have a very large sheet of paper, and extra paper handy, you will be fine. This is not about perfection or looking pretty. You simply need something to write on and a way to organize the different jobs.

Positive		Negative
	Job 1	
	Job 2	
	Job 3	

It is important to make a separate row where you have had a drastically different emotional experience. For example, I have been a video editor for individual clients in my freelance business, and a video editor for a national TV news station. These should be two different sections even though the technical task or title was the same. They were very different experiences for me, happened at two different points in my life, and my salary was even different.

Once you have written down one job, put the general year and length of time you spent at that job, next to it for reference. Also list generally how much money you made from that job. These numbers will help you later on in the assignment.

Under that same job listing and date, on the left you are going to write everything about that job that you liked, enjoyed, or found rewarding. Essentially, anything positive about the job goes to the left of that center line. On the other half, for that same job listing, you will write all the things you hated, disliked or generally had negative feelings towards.

Positive		Negative
Job 1		
Teaching		Long Commute
Producing & Editing- Variety	Dates	No Benefits
Trusted to Lead	Salary	Temporary Job
Creative Flexibility		Stressful Schedule
Learning		Heavy Lifting/Physical
Job 2		
Editing, fast paced		Lazy Coworkers
Teaching		No Promotion/Growth
Social Environment	Dates	Disliked Content
Drive to Work	Salary	Long Hours, Sitting All Day
Title		Not Challenging or Creative
Health Benefits		No Variety
Job 3		
Easy, Social Environment		Low Pay
Creative at times		Long Commute
Benefits	Dates	Bureaucracy, No Growth
Some Teaching	Salary	Micromanager
Flexible Schedule		Not Challenging, Boring
Producing & Editing & Photography		Heavy Lifting

For example, my list for my current freelance position might say teaching, and more time for exercise on the positive side. The negative side would say unpredictable hours and isolation of working from home.

Write down at least three for each job, and be specific. In my case, unpredictable hours causes me to have less time for social events, and an increased anxiety because I do not know my schedule more than a week in advance. Don't just list a feeling, write down the measurable action or attribute that caused you to feel that way.

Once you've done this for all the jobs and experiences you've had, it is important for you to see that every job has had positive and negative. We are not comparing the overall experience of the jobs to one another. This is not a ratings scale of what is better, although you certainly will have more positives than negatives in some places. That's fine. If we were just looking at a ratings scale, we would start to feel like our best days are behind us. That is not the case.

Ideal Positives

Teaching
Flexible Schedule
Producing, Editing, Photography
Variety
Creative
Drive to Work
Learning
Leader

Deal-Breakers

Long Commute
Heavy Lifting
Sitting all day/Long Hours

Ideal Job Checklist:

Is this job creative enough?
Do I believe in this content? Or at least, does it fit within my beliefs?
Is there an opportunity for autonomy and creativity?
Can I see myself commuting to this location daily?
Do I feel comfortable asking for work/life balance in this position?

In this exercise, the goal is to break each job down into minor tasks, activities and attributes. Then, we will look at just the positive column for attributes that repeat. We're looking for patterns. Most of my jobs have involved teaching, and I would always list that as a positive aspect.

Make one completely new list. This will be your Ideal Career Assessment. On the positive side, we are listing all the repeated words or common themes we found in that column from the Past Career Assessment. Do the same for the negative side. Underneath those lists write out a checklist for yourself that will guide you in applying to new jobs.

What are the must-haves that are necessary for you to meet all of them, in order to take on this new opportunity? This will be a unique list for you based on your previous patterns. Here is a look at mine.

This Ideal Career Assessment is important to keep handy when searching for a job because that negative column serves as a deal-breaker list for you. If you are applying to a job that lists more than a few of these deal-breakers, you know it's not going to be right. This list of what we don't want in a future career is going to be much easier to make because we have already been in the situation. We have had the negative experience and felt the effects of it first-hand, well enough to know we never want to do it again.

> *"I think I was 20, I had my own office and I was in charge of the mid-west sales for Astralwerks. It was just like, first of all, who put me in charge of that? I don't know why. I'm glad they believed in me [but] I didn't really believe in me at the time. I quit that job five times. I just kept showing back up the next day. I don't know why. The main reason was I would go in, I would quit and the last thing my boss would say to me is, 'You're being foolish because people would kill to get their foot in the door right now and you're in. What are you doing?' I would let that pressure me into thinking like that, because I wasn't sleeping. I was working sometimes fifteen hour days. I was trying to get my own business off the ground. I didn't see my friends and family. I had just graduated college. I had no idea what was going on. I wasn't reflecting at all. I was just going, going, going because this was the goal.*
>
> *The goal was to work in the music industry. I have this job, that's all that matters. I wasn't taking time, honestly, I was too afraid to stop and say, is this what I want? Because I*

just spent four years getting to this point, what if I found out it wasn't what I wanted? Which ultimately, it wasn't."
-Suzanne Paulinski: Mindset Coach for
Musicians & Industry Professionals

"[At my past corporate job] They'd give you free dinner and a free car ride home if you stayed late. The perks of investment banking, I saw it firsthand. Every place I worked, people wanted to hire me because I'm a person who gets bored doing nothing. I always said No. They're like, 'Why not?'... [because] I'm an artist, I'm a singer, I'm an actress.

I'll never forget, I rode a car home with somebody from Goldman Sachs one night. The guy in the car was talking all about how he makes this six figure income and his family and his wife and the pressures, but what he really wanted to do was be a high school math teacher. He couldn't wait to retire from investment banking and have a second career. He had been in investment banking for 30 years. At that moment, I said to myself, you're going to have to work hard at anything you want to do. You might as well work hard at something you love.

Right there was the moment that I was like, I will not settle. I am not going to live a life of accepting these job offers that people want to give me. I don't necessarily think that anybody who makes that choice is a bad person or even a sellout. I just knew for myself, if I made that choice, that I would get very, very comfortable with a lot of money very quickly and my life would be all about that. All about being this guy's assistant, being there at 7 o'clock in the morning and leaving at 7 o'clock at night. That's

not how I want to spend my life. I'm really glad because I definitely wouldn't have gotten the chance to sing at Carnegie Hall if I stayed working [in that corporate job]."
-Julia Amisano: Singing, Piano & Acting Teacher

"It's important to have those experiences where you realize 'this is not for me'. At the same time, not to just say NO but to acknowledge WHY NOT? If you just say no then in your mind, this experience or this label, it's shut off for years to come. Yet if you say that's something for when I have more money or something for when I'm not working on my business or when I have kids, or don't have kids, or whatever it might be. It's very important to know that, to name it and claim it, and to know why not."
-Brett Solomano: Hollywood Stuntman, Author, Speaker and Coach

The positive side of this column might have a lot less written down, or a lot more. This is your unique list. Most of us tend to remember negative emotions more strongly, so it might come to mind faster to fill out the negative side. Think really hard about every aspect of your past job and try to find even the tiniest positive. Perhaps you liked your desk, your office, your commute was easy, or you enjoyed having holidays off. These details are more important than you think because they are lifestyle choices. Keep in mind the overall positives and what is a must-have, when you are making your checklist.

"What really out of all of those things speaks to you the most, fulfills you the most? Of all those things you do, when you're performing them, makes you forget about the time? Where you look up at the clock and four hours has gone by and you

didn't even know it. Which of those things can you stay up until 2am doing and you wouldn't even mind. Those are the things that you need to pay attention to. That's obviously having an effect on you that you need to dial in and focus on."
-Alex Wood, co-founder of HoneLife
and the Variety Seeker Tribe

"Some people get into the state of thinking, when they're trying to play guitar or dance, etc. You can't play A grade stuff when you're thinking. It's got to come from within... The more you can capture these moments, the more you can get into that state of flow. Maybe you're having a fantastic conversation with someone, and everything is going right. Or for me, driving my truck, I spend so much time driving trucks for stunts- that's the place where I'm the most comfortable, especially at high speeds it's just something that the faster I go, the more comfortable I am. Whether you're on stage or trying to create, perform, play something, I think you really have to focus on not focusing, and allowing it to flow through. That's where the word FLOW comes from. You're not thinking, not channeling not filtering it. You're just trying to observe it, and sitting on the sidelines spectating as it kind of comes through."
-Brett Solomano: Hollywood Stuntman,
Author, Speaker and Coach

Flow is a common theme mentioned in a lot of self-help books and articles about productivity and success. Of course, we like doing things that we have done in the past because we are confident in our ability to deliver. Is that task easy but mundane and you are so bored of it? Or is it something that gets us in a state of flow because we feel confident and sure that we are doing the thing we are meant to be doing each day? If there are things you didn't mind doing but don't particularly care for, don't write them on your list. Make sure to put a star next to the major flow points of each experience, and look for repetition of these flow points from job to job. We definitely want to be challenged and have things we aspire to, so "potential for growth" might be on that list, but we don't flow when we have the "potential for growth." You will find specific flow points that are task-related, not based on feelings or possibilities. Be detailed about your list of positives and it will tell you a lot about yourself.

My own assessment lists video editing on the positive side, which is a solo task. But it also lists social interaction, which for me is meeting new people and having coworkers to bounce ideas off of. These two preferences of mine may seem contradictory, but it helps me eliminate jobs that are missing one of the two key elements. The patterns on the positive side of your list will guide you in finding your ideal job. Whereas the negatives from the other side which will make up your list of deal-breakers.

> "Listen to oneself own advice. You are the expert of your own life but you have to find the space to listen to your own voice. So you have to take a pause and reflect. It would be nice if you could do it at the end of the day because why do we brush our teeth every day- why can't we do this to our own mental health. Empty out all the doubts, all the worries at the end of the day and put on a fresh face. We have to put on fresh clothes. You can't always look back that woulda coulda shoulda, because it will stick in our minds. Always be letting go of our old notion of ourselves, to be courageous to face the future because everything will be fine. We have so much competence, so much talent but we just have to find the time and space."
> –Alma-Villegas Schwalbenberg, PHD

It can be really scary to imagine leaving your current job for another, or to completely change your field of work. Sometimes the scariest thing might be confusion. Your list might be all over the place, making you feel even more unsure. That is okay. Take some time to process all of this. It is a big assignment and does not have to be done in one sitting. Reflect on it and know that you are worthy of having an amazing career.

If you're not sure what you want to do next, but just know that what you've been doing is not right... you might have to think as far back as your childhood.

"Journalism has been a love of mine since I was 12 years old. For me it feels like forever. I had this really awesome teacher in middle school and he gave us this homework to write an essay as if you were a music journalist. He gave us all numbers to pick out of, and each number was an album. I chose Metallica. That was the first time I got into journalism, through him. I learned how to write about music- because he used to write for MTV before he became a teacher, so he always put that aspect of journalism in his teaching. So I really fell in love with that whole process of listening to an album, critiquing it, breaking it down and I got a perfect score on that essay. This was fun, I really like this."
-Mayra Ramales: Founder &
Manager of theSoundLive.com

"When I was twenty, I was like, 'I'm going to give myself until I'm 30 to figure out what I want to do.' I think that there's a lot of pressure to know what you want to do right out of high school. 'What's your major?' I think that there's a lot of fear in that pressure, societal fear. It's important to ignore that and take your time and explore and figure out what your skills and your passions and the environment you want to

be in and people you want to work with, and find what gels in all of those respects. I was a photographer in high school. I went to City College for cinematography. Then I randomly took one more internship after grad school [where] I was the receptionist at a post house. I got a glimpse into that world and was really drawn to color correction for the photography relationship." -Janis Vogel: Professional TV & Film Editor

"I've been performing since I was little. If you asked me at six years old, what do you want to be, in fact, people did ask me. I'd be like, 'I want to be a singer.' They'd be like, 'What else do you want to be?' I was so confused by that. I was like, 'I want to be an astronaut.' Then they just stopped talking and walked away. I wanted to be a singer anyway. That's my first answer and I'm sticking to it."
-Julia Amisano: Singing, Piano & Acting Teacher

Not every passion we had as a child works as a career, but if you see a pattern in your positive list that corresponds to hobbies you enjoyed as a child- that is usually a good sign that you are on the right path. After all, if we are willing to do these assignments just for the fun of it with no monetary gain, then certainly adding a paycheck on top of that would not be too shabby. I used to do photo shoots with my friends back in high school and as early as middle school. I found it really enjoyable to set up lighting, poses and think about composition. Today I use those skills every day in my video production business. Some skills are instinctual and others we learn through practice. Don't discredit the work you did for fun. You might not list it on a resume but it certainly could help you in the long-run.

"I love performing at churches because I have a musical background. I grew up in the church and choirs so when I perform at churches it allows me to really have fun because I have access to things I don't normally have in a comedy club. There's an organ there, there's a drum there, so I can incorporate music within my comedy which is really fun."
-Angela Star: Comedian

Remember that the form is just as important as the task itself. You will notice that on your list. For example, my list says autonomy quite a few times as a positive aspect of certain jobs. This is why it is important to be specific when creating your list. Filmmaking is a group effort which I enjoy doing occasionally. On a daily basis though, it does not provide me enough autonomy. I like to do the bulk of the work and be responsible for the final product, even if my part is a minor contribution to a larger project. This is a pattern I can see even when thinking back into my childhood.

I always dreaded group assignments because I like to be in charge, and when paired with someone who doesn't like being in charge, I end up doing a much larger portion of the work assignment. This can sometimes lead to resentment, but it is usually my own fault because I failed to ask for help or be assertive enough to assign tasks clearly. Applying this knowledge to my ideal career, I can see that in past projects I did enjoy working with clients to collaborate. Another form of filmmaking that has worked for me is broadcast journalism or documentary work. The act of filmmaking is the same: operating cameras, editing, producing. However, the form is different because I am usually by myself or in a much smaller team where everyone has a very specific role, and those roles do not overlap. Certainly, you can identify some of these forms versus tasks in your own list, and be more specific to help you find clarity. The key is to not deny your personality. Accept what is unique to you, be it your prefer-ence for control or maybe you're more laid back. Perhaps you like to socialize all day, or you prefer to be alone. Whatever it is for you, accept that, and mold your career to accommodate it.

Let's think again about the formula: *Action x Perspective = Feelings*. We remember bad experiences so much more vividly than good ones. Certainly, bad memories are much more powerful than neutral experiences which we might forget completely. Just because something is on your negative list as a pattern doesn't mean it belongs there forever. You have changed drastically throughout your life. Your perspective can have a huge impact on any negative feeling or activity you do. For example, if you're in a job with friends you love spending time with, where every day feels fun and joyous, you might not mind doing a mundane task repeatedly. It is a multiply symbol, not addition. So, if you have a completely negative perspective (a zero), even if the outside circumstance is good, you might still feel like a zero. If you can get your perspective in a good state, the negative tasks won't have as much of an impact.

I say this to encourage you to remember the importance of your perspective in any situation. Also, to realize that you were in a very different emotional state for each job you've had. You were focusing on either the positive or the negative. If the overall positives outweigh the negatives, you probably spent more time at that job (or would not have minded staying longer). If the negatives were so unbearable with little reprise from the positive aspects of the job, you likely weren't there very long. Now that we are separated from that experience, it is easier to step back and look at how our attitude (good or bad) contributed to it.

Our environment can play a huge role in our mindset and the way we feel about a job. When thinking about your ideal lifestyle, ask yourself what type of environment you prefer to be in each day. Make sure to have this aspect of the setting, as part of your list for each role, and notice what worked best for you. I definitely prefer to have a solitary space when editing, but I also want to have variation in my daily setting to avoid feeling isolated and lonely. I dislike open floor plans or spaces where you can hear every little noise. It is distracting for a video editor, and doesn't work for me all the time. Realistically, a mix of the two environments would be my ideal. As a freelancer I have variety in my setting since I work from home and travel to clients, and that works for me, but I spend more time isolated than I would like.

> *"I think one of the things I always grappled with was, do I want to be outside or do I want to be inside? Nature or the cave? The cave won in the end, which I'm surprised about. You can find solitude but you can also have a crazy party in a cave. I think in some ways it's both more stable and more versatile. You get to have your solitary time but you're an integral part of bringing a film or story to life. I love that aspect of it because I love having a room full of creative people and all discussing how to craft this thing. I love having my quiet time to just do all of that. There are a lot of things that determine what you want to do and what works best."*
> *-Janis Vogel: Professional TV & Film Editor*

Health is another really important factor to focus on when creating your list. The internship I had for two years in college was physically demanding on me to carry heavy cameras and lights all around New York City. It is possible that I herniated discs in my back during this time. Or perhaps it was the editing job I had right after, where I used to sit down for ten hours a day for more than a year. Maybe it was one of the next jobs where I did a mix of lifting heavy equipment and sitting for long periods of time. Or maybe one of the times I slipped in the snow. Perhaps it was all of these things. There is no way to know what caused me to have severe back pain for years, so I don't dwell on it, but I do take it into consideration when making lifestyle choices.

The six years I spent at the last university job I had, were a good indication to me that my career choice was not healthy. The same year I won an Emmy award, I found myself in bed for the better part of four months recovering from a knee injury. The medication was so strong that I could barely get out of bed. I missed a lot of work and my responsibilities were changed to where I had even more time being isolated in the office, because I couldn't carry equipment or do much traveling. I was given less assignments, and I felt like a failure. The prescription medication probably exacerbated my depression and feelings of worthlessness. I'll save that story for another book on the wonders of natural remedies.

At the time, I was not physically or mentally healthy. I hated my job now because I had been relegated to watch as everyone else does all the assignments I wanted to do. This experience really pushed me to reevaluate my life. Yes, this university job even before the injury was easy for me. Paid well, benefits, doing what I studied, but the lifestyle was not correct. I was commuting during rush hour into NYC to sit at a desk for eight hours and eat junk food all day because I was bored with my lack of assignments. When I made my list of things I wanted from the ideal job, I knew even back then that I wanted to drive to work. I wanted the option to telecommute at times, and set my own schedule so I could incorporate exercise into my daily routine. I wanted variety in my everyday tasks. Here I am today writing a book, something I could not have done in that negative state, inflicted upon me by the wrong lifestyle.

> *"Dance is my first love. It's my therapy as well. I did it for a while and was pursuing it professionally, and realizing what my body can and can't do. I didn't like the audition process. I started to hate it. It was cattle calls, and I just couldn't pursue it professionally because it's my therapy, it's my joy. So I dance now for fun and classes. It relieves that pressure. I got into film because I had an injury when I was doing a show. I pulled my hamstring but still had to perform*

*with it, so it got worse, and damaged it really bad. Now it's
healed but I realized with film that I can love it so much
but still pursue it in a business-sense. I couldn't do that with
dance. I still miss being on stage but now I just do it for fun."*
— *Gabrielle Aliké Hawkins: Filmmaker*

I had to make a major career shift back then, and decide that
I cannot be a videographer and editor full-time without accom-
modations. It honestly felt like I was mourning the death of my
career. It was tough, but I realized over time that it is all about
balance. With the right lifestyle choices that I have at this time,
I can balance teaching with video production to create the right
mix for me. Still though, I make sure to not lift heavy equipment
the way I used to. I ask for help when I need it, and avoid situations where I might aggravate my back. Sometimes we realize that
we just cannot physically do the things we are used to doing. No
matter what age, our bodies are precious and delicate. We need to
treat them with care, and listen to them when they are telling us
something is not right. There is nothing like an injury to force us
into thinking clearly about our life choices.

*"I've had my physical hurdles. I have a scoliosis and I have
tendonitis in my hips. I think it's just important to try to
foster the physical capabilities that you do have. If you can
stand for a little while each day, that's great. Whatever
your range of motion is, try to keep that up. That's challenging. It's really challenging as an editor. Actually,
one of the things that really helped motivate me was
FitnessinPost.com. I don't want to say that everybody
should be running three miles a day. People have limitations.
Whatever you can do for your well-being, whether it's dietary
or meditation or physical activities, it's all really important."*
— *Janis Vogel: Professional TV & Film Editor*

With lifestyle in mind, take a look at your Past Career Assessment list again. Since it was done in chronological order, write down or circle on the negative side what caused you to leave each job. Not just the reason you tell potential employers, but truly what was the straw that broke the camel's back and really pushed you to leave that job? The answer could be physical, mental, or a mix of both. If you see patterns, consider potential deal breakers in your Ideal Career Assessment list.

"Before I became an art therapist I was in a business career. It was very different. I worked in the corporate world for many years, and I was not aware of what art therapy is. Even though art had been part of my life since I was a little kid. I had used journaling, art and drawing all my life. My parents were very creative. I was not satisfied in the business field. I was pretty much miserable with the whole mentality of corporate. Not to get too personal- but I had a loss in the family, and I was faced with grief. This significant loss gave me a chance to get in touch with my art. I remember doing that first painting with charcoal, and I was like 'Oh my God- this is exactly what I wanted to express'. There were no words. I remember just like yesterday, it was a window I had drawn out of charcoal and I added paint to it. In that moment I asked what is this? Painting can be so powerful. In that moment I knew I had to do more of this.

It's very hard to explain when you feel something try to transform you internally through art. You feel it in your body that it's happening, and you feel your mind gaining some clarity and space. You just feel it... I did painting for a couple of years and started going to art school. I did a lot of research into how art heals. Then I discovered art therapy and I decided- This is it! This is my calling. I felt

it in myself how art made me heal, and I want to help
other people with the same thing. So I quit my corporate
job and put all my efforts into becoming an art therapist."
-Arta Cakaj, MS, LCAT: Wholehearted Art Therapy

This exercise is not to judge how much time we've wasted, but how being put in certain situations have helped us grow and learn a lesson. You might notice a pattern of burnout on your list of reasons why. Perhaps you were overly stressed by working a certain amount of hours, or juggling too many responsibilities between your job and home life. Mental health is just as important as physical health. What can you learn from these lessons?

We all could do much more for ourselves in the self-care category. Was there a gap in-between certain experiences that helped you recharge? If so, what did you do specifically that helped? Having a vacation is great but sometimes all we need is a good massage or a mental health day at home. Find the activities outside of work that help you recharge, and don't forget to take a break now and then. Sometimes I am so caught up in my projects that I forget to eat, I may go to bed too late, or don't get up from the chair enough to stretch. Since I started freelancing I've had a lot less social time, less time and money for traveling, and have to make an effort to reach out to my friends to schedule fun. It was never this hard when I had a job I didn't like. Remember that life is not just about work and achieving goals, we have to enjoy it as well to avoid letting exhaustion confuse our body's stress receptors.

"I guess I've always been attracted to jobs that show me
different parts of the world. I love meeting new people and
seeing through that, new ideas and how people live. I'm just
fascinated by how people live and the fears they have, the
experiences they have. The dreams, the desires, all that kind
of stuff. So, I've been really blessed to see something like 30

different states in the past couple of years since I've been here [in the US]. Most of it getting paid to do it as well, just working with a fireworks company and truck driving, and exploring the US through the eyes of festival goers. Also, I'm always taking a bit of time off, making sure I can squeeze a day or two in the city, wherever I might be whether it's New York, Cleveland, Indiana, or Vegas. It's always great to see it through the eyes of the locals. I don't like doing touristy stuff."
                          –Brett Solomano: Hollywood Stuntman,
                                Author, Speaker and Coach

If you are thinking about a complete career change, don't be overwhelmed. You are not the first person to do so. Many people at various ages have left their long-term jobs in search of something new. It is never too late.

"I used to think that– I spent so many years studying business, economics and management– all that time is wasted. Why couldn't I have done this when I was 25 years old, or earlier? The truth is, whatever you learn in life has a purpose. You will use it at some point. All those skills that you learn, somehow, they will come to your advantage. I used to separate my business world with my artistic and creative world, like it's just two parts of the brain. Truth is that if you learn how to integrate these two worlds together, you will be a better person.

As far as advice, it's very personal. As long as you go after what your passion is, and what you really believe in… I always go back to that when things get difficult. Running a business is like a wave. Sometimes you'll be high and sometimes low. You have to go with that. I feel grounded when I know that is my calling and my purpose. Why am I doing what I'm doing? So, I always go to what I'm passionate about and why I'm doing this work in the world. That just helps me feel grounded and feel like all this hard work that I'm doing has a reason. I'm doing this because I love what I do and I'm passionate about helping people. I'm passionate about my work.

Finances come around and sometimes hold us back from going for our dream. We find different reasons like I can't do this because of that. Sometimes they are real challenges because it's hard to switch careers, especially when you are already successful in one career but you're not happy with that. It's really about what drives you. What is it inside of you that makes you want to get out of bed and really make a difference? Something you won't get tired of. Not to say it's not challenging, it is challenging but once you find what you're really passionate about, then everything else sort of finds its way. Just do some soul searching of what drives you and what makes you happy. What helps you get up in the morning to feel motivated?"
-Arta Cakaj, MS, LCAT: Wholehearted Art Therapy

As creatives, a lot of us struggle with perfectionism. For those of us who also have curiosity and seek variety, it can be really tough to narrow down a single path. I am the type of person who likes to know how things work. For example, I might want to take apart a television to see how the inside pieces work together to give us moving images, but that doesn't mean I want to become a person who builds TVs. For me, sometimes just the knowledge is enough to satisfy my curiosity. It doesn't always lead to a life-long or even long-term project or goal. Similarly, I find it so important to try things out before committing to something long term.

"I got into photography through my old director at LaGuardia, who got me into meeting all of these people and working. He was the one who told me to buy a camera, and start doing it on your own... I'm self taught in photography. I never took any classes, never majored in photography... The best way to learn is to put yourself in it and try it out, test it and see how it works. That's how you grow."
—Mayra Ramales: Founder &
Manager of theSoundLive.com

When we are working somewhere less than ideal, just the thought of a shiny new job is exciting and we get blinded by the salary, the benefits and the excitement. We aren't thinking about the everyday logistics of how this is going to work, or even if this is right for us. Eight years ago, after graduating college in New York and being severely burned out from working, I was offered a job with a higher title and more money, but it was in Massachusetts. It required me to move away from my family and friends in the only city I had ever lived in, and leave my full time position. At the time, it felt like the right thing to do because I was just sick of the same routine that was not working for me. I was so excited about this opportunity for change that I missed the signs that would have warned me against working for this volatile and financially unstable company. Thinking back, I see red flags for potential personality conflicts with that former manager as early as our first interview, but I ignored them.

"It's a skill we have as human beings, to be able to perceive something in the future and latch on. I think that gets us stuck. We often think that's what I want, and we grab on to the thought or the vision or the action too early. We don't step into it. We don't just even sit there and consider it for a little longer. When we do, it's that we want to plan, plan and then we never take action. So I think our

mind often trips us up. School, for better or worse, doesn't teach us how to reach into what I call our 'not-past'. Meaning, we can always do things from our past, which is showing up in the same way every day. But what would it look like to show up and step into something that you haven't done before? Something not from your past? We're never taught that habit. We never practice that."
-Brett Solomano: Hollywood Stuntman,
Author, Speaker and Coach

I had to learn that lesson yet again when I left my six-year university job to work at another college. I was so excited about the opportunity to have a higher title and honestly, to try something new, that I totally missed a big red flag about the position that caused me to leave just one month later. Even though it didn't work out the way I expected, the experience was the kick in the butt I needed to finally start freelancing. After two years of researching and asking everyone I know about the benefits of entrepreneurship, I was still too scared to have left the cocoon that was my old job. Sometimes it's good to jump into a new experience with all your faith and hope. Trying something new could be exactly what you need to make a much-needed change in your life. It could lead you to your true calling. So, even though you may learn the same lesson again and again, the message might be different. Look for those big impact situations in your life as a way to grow. Focus on the details and how you can make the best of it.

"One school in Bed Stuy Brooklyn asked me to come for career day. I was the only one who was a comedian. Everyone else was a firefighter, police officer, the cool things. They introduced me as the clown. I was able to come in and relate with the kids, just make jokes and it seemed like it was the most fulfilling day that I had. To be able to go

from class to class and they just loved me and we were
able to relate. I felt like them because I remember being
that age and wishing that I could just express myself and
be normal and not have to be like everyone. That sparked
the idea for me to work with kids on a regular basis."
-Angela Star: Comedian

As demonstrated from Angela's story, trying something out of your normal routine might spark an idea you never had before. An experience like this, which gives you such an incredible feeling, would make your ideal career positives list. Since you already know how good it feels to be surrounded by kids, for example, now it's time to dig deeper. From there, any little negative would help you narrow down specifics of HOW you would want to work with kids. For Angela, this experience led her to start a program called "Stars of Comedy" where she teaches kids about comedy. Working with kids is hard, believe me I know, and it is not for everyone. The key here is how this new experience made Angela feel, and how it inspired her to keep going in this direction. Use these important moments of clarity to fuel your fire and motivate you towards success. It's not magic though- You have to put in the work if you want to make a major change in your career. Often this means starting from scratch in a new field. John Trigonis' advice about crowdfunding can be applied here.

"You've got to put your all in each one. There are still people
that will launch a campaign and let it sit there and they
expect, like the campaign is a seed for a money tree. You
put it there. You post it one time on Twitter, Facebook, and
your e-mail list. Then you come back two months later and
you're fully funded. You might as well believe in the tooth
fairy and just yank out all your teeth and shove them under
your pillow. It doesn't happen. You've got to work. You've

got to hoe that field. You've got to cultivate it and grow that on your own. You've got to sweat. You've just gotta put in that work. Even if you put in that work, the crops may die. It just might not work. Then you gotta do it all over again. Just like that movie 'The Martian'. You'll never know what's going to happen. Something's going to kill all your crops and you've got to start from scratch. That's the reality."
−John T. Trigonis: Filmmaker, Poet & Indiegogo's
Head Film and Creative Campaign Strategist

When you have your list of ideal positives and negatives for your next career move, you can start thinking about potential avenues to explore. It can be difficult to know what is the right next move for us. Listen to that inner voice to find your next move, think about your ideal lifestyle, and make sure to incorporate your WHY. It's up to you to keep pushing in that new direction, work hard and reflect on your experience throughout the process. After all, whatever decision you make is just a jumping off point. Nothing lasts forever, and you can change your mind later on.

This list has helped me make very important decisions in my life. I hope it works for you as well in finding your ideal career path. Remember your career is a journey not a destination. We are never done working, if our work is a reflection of who we are.

CHAPTER 9

MONEY, MONEY, MONEY

While you still have your list from the last chapter handy, check out the salary numbers you listed next to each job. Then ask yourself, did the salary correspond in any way to the positive or negative value of the job? It might have made a difference in how long you spent there, but did it make the job feel any better to make more money? Probably not. The opposite might be true though. Did the lack of money make it difficult to continue working there?

The thing to focus on is whether the higher paying jobs caused you to have a more positive experience overall. The answer is usually NO. For me, starting out as a freelancer I noticed quickly that my income was radically different each month. Sometimes I made just about as much as I did when working full-time. Other months I made significantly less. Measuring my income monthly makes me very anxious, especially because payments are not regularly scheduled and it might take months to get payment for a gig. The better way to calculate my income is by quarter, or every four months because I get an average that is much more comfortable to look at.

When you think about going freelance or leaving your 9-to-5, there are other things to consider besides the salary. While I may be making less money some months, I am saving significantly in transportation fees, and I am saving by not buying expensive lunches in Manhattan each day. Numbers aside, my improved health and happiness is worth more to me than making a few extra dollars.

Let's take a look at what people have to say about freelance income as compared to full time income from a traditional 9-to-5. Do they make more or less money as a freelancer?

> *"I have made more as a freelancer than if I were full time. At advertising agencies, the prevalence of working overtime at time and a half rates means nearly anyone freelance makes more than the staff. The caveat to that is most freelancers choose not to work 50 weeks a year. There is a high rate of burnout. In the entertainment industry, there is so much variation in pay that it's an impossible question to answer."*
> *–Diana Cherkas: Freelance Actor, Writer,*
> *Advertising Copywriter & Copy Editor*

> *"I'd say about the same. Hour for hour I'm working far more I would say. Though the results and fulfillment speak for themselves. If all goes according to plan I could let the business run itself where I would just keep plugging ideas in to it and I wouldn't have to worry about the income side of things anymore." –Brett Solomano: Hollywood Stuntman, Author, Speaker and Coach*

> *"Less, but it's worth it. Plus, I don't have the burden of travel expense and the time it takes to get to and from work."*
> *–Elaine Del Valle: Film & TV*
> *Director, Producer & Actress*

> *"Less [but] It's worth it because I don't like being told what to do, or more importantly when/how to do it. That's priceless."*
> *–Suzanne Paulinski: Mindset Coach for*
> *Musicians & Industry Professionals*

"Working as a freelancer offers the potential to increase your income because every time you start somewhere new, you have the opportunity to negotiate. This process is what you make of it however, and understanding the scope of work before accepting a job can certainly impact how much money you think you deserve and whether compensation is commensurate with your yearly salary goals."
–Anonymous survey participant
(Freelance TV/Film Editor)

The shift, if and when you become a freelancer, is that you have to assume you will not work as many hours as you did when full time. The money is just not as consistent. You are not guaranteed anything. If you don't have a project to work on, or don't have a client you can bill for hours worked, you are not getting paid. I am no longer waiting out the clock until 5pm, on the company dime. No more detention for me. Now I am getting paid for every moment I work. There are also hours of work that go into freelancing and entrepreneurship that are unpaid, like marketing, consultations or looking for your next gig. Your hourly rate has to reflect this. You will have to charge more for freelance hours than you did as a full time worker. This gives potential to make more money in a good month, and balance out for the months you make less.

"[As a freelancer, I make] more probably. The secret- I overload myself. I work late into the night. 14 hour days are the norm. That way I can make 1.5x or twice my rate in one day, especially because I work faster."
–Billy Nawrocki: Freelance
Filmmaker & Video Editor

I have also found that I work faster as a freelancer because I am not distracted by being in an open office space with coworkers.

There is much less socializing which means I am more focused on my task. Also, I am learning that the faster I can get at each task, the more money I can potentially make because I have increased my available hours. As I mentioned before, this added focus comes with a lack of social interaction. It is certainly a trade-off.

Of course, becoming a freelancer has a lot of expenses too, not just income. When we have a sick day, or take a vacation, we lose money because there is no paid time off. We have to pay for office supplies, office space and all of the things we need to do our job. For creatives in the photography or video business, expenses can be very high. On video shoots, it is expected that I will show up with a huge camera and crew. Depending on the project though, it might just be me with a mirrorless 4k camera that cost me less than $1000 but shoots footage that looks great because I have studied the craft of photography for years. Sometimes it's not about the camera, but the lens. There are websites out there for people who want to rent a lens for a day, or a week for much less than the cost of purchasing new. You could also try buying something used or refurbished. Having a good photo is more about the lighting than the camera, so updating the camera body each year is not necessary. I purchased a very expensive light kit on ebay for just a few hundred dollars because it was used.

> "When you do anything related to photography or film, you're gonna spend a lot of money. It's just an expensive hobby. I think that's just something you should expect... I wouldn't say you should go out though and buy all these expensive lenses. If you're not gonna profit off of it then you're really just wasting money. A lot of it is style and what you learn. It's not about how much your lens costs. It's based on you, your vision, your style. You make that photo."
> –Mayra Ramales: Founder &
> Manager of theSoundLive.com

"It's all perception. [People assume that] If it looks good, then it has to be expensive. Money is a really big way that people get in their own way. There are millions of dreams that are dying right now, literally dying because people think they need to have this wad of cash like Scrooge McDuck to start their business."
— Temica Gross: Budget Business Coach

Surely whatever field you work in, you can find used or refurbished items, or consider renting rather than buying new. Look around for those deals. No matter what field you're in, buy what you NEED to get the job done, not the fancy new gadget that will be outdated in a few months. A lot of people love to get the brand-new phone that comes out each year. Do you really need to spend money on that? Or would you rather put that money into a savings account and after five years have enough for a down payment on a new car? If you are going to invest in your business, look into a small business loan for large purchases. Again, make sure you are only buying what is necessary.

Unfortunately, in today's society we DO have to think about making enough money to meet our personal expenses. Not every expense is business-related. While health and happiness are priceless, there are still bills to pay. Life happens. Cars break down, we might need to move, our partner might need help, or surprise- an unexpected child comes into your life. There are unlimited things that could potentially happen which will require money. The longer you spend "saving" with no goal in mind, the more time you are wasting. The more potential money-sucking events that can occur, and quickly you can realize that five, ten or twenty years of your life was wasted trying to save money. This is the reason that knowing your WHY is so important. Set goals that are value based, because we will never have enough money in the bank. It is important to have savings for a rainy day, but don't let life's everyday surprises spring up on you and put your dreams on the back burner.

> *"The thoughts of never creating or generate enough income...*
> *I've put that behind me a long time ago that it's not about*
> *the dollars and cents. Obviously, you want to travel and eat*
> *and do the things you want to do... You can build a lifestyle*
> *around doing what you want without having to be rich.*
> *Even if you want these mansions and millions of dollars,*
> *what these rich people have let us know is that even once*
> *they have acquired these things, there's still a void within*
> *them. It doesn't fulfill them the way they want to be fulfilled."*
> *–Alex Wood, co-founder of HoneLife*
> *and the Variety Seeker Tribe*

> *"It doesn't mean that if you're famous and you have*
> *money, that you're going to have a good life. It's a dis-*
> *traction, [we are paying attention to celebrities] and*
> *it's a way that we forget about real problems that are*
> *happening in the world- kids starving every day and wars."*
> *–Michelle Engberg: Professional Photographer*

If you're chasing fame, that's one thing. Go for it. Sometimes fame can mean a platform that can help you shed light on important issues. To each his own. If you are chasing money, I don't recommend it because you will be running for a long time. Make sure to set a goal number. Otherwise if you just want more, more, more, you will never have enough. Perhaps you want money to buy a house. Why do you want a house? Is a house the best thing for your lifestyle? I would rather live in a smaller apartment if it means I don't have to shovel snow or take out heavy garbage each week. Also, living smaller means you can have less expenses, which means less worry about working long hours, or finding that next gig. There comes a time when we have to really reconsider how much money we spend, and change our habits. How much money do you need to live the life you really want?

We all want to be working consistently and enjoying our job, but as freelancers I can tell you it is not guaranteed that we will have a job lined up each week, or even tomorrow. The money is usually not consistent. If you want the freedom of freelance, it is worth exploring how to reduce your expenses, just in case. Even a full time worker does not have a guarantee that they will be employed tomorrow. It is a good idea to reduce your expenses, so you can reach your goal faster. Expenses I am speaking of include rent or mortgage, cable TV, cell phone bill, car loans, debt repayment and those monthly subscriptions that quickly add up. There are ways we can reduce or eliminate most of these. Separate your must-haves from your luxury items. The luxury items can be shopped around for. For example, I don't NEED cable tv, this is a luxury. To lower my monthly expenses, I might switch to a different plan that costs less money, or eliminate cable all together in exchange for a streaming service that costs less. When it comes to the bills we need to pay, like our cell phone plan, look at your monthly usage compared to how much you are paying for. If there is a less expensive plan that will work for you, that is a definite way to save money. Maybe we are paying for up to 2GB of data but never use more than 1GB. In that case, inquire with your cell phone company, and competing companies, about a plan that better suits you. Also, with all of your bills, ask for discounts that are related to the places you work, community you live in, groups you are a part of, or based on your income. Most cell phone carriers, gyms, utility and cable providers provide discounts. They don't advertise discounts. You have to ask for them.

Our loans and debt can be refinanced for lower rates usually, or combined. I read a book about credit and debt by Suze Orman a few years ago and it helped me get my credit score in very good shape. The key for me is to always carry a zero balance on my credit cards.

Why give the credit card companies extra money when you could just pay them back at the end of the month? I use an Amazon.com credit card for most of my purchases because it has 3% cash back on all purchases, and 5% cash back if shopping through Amazon (which is where I do most of my buying). So, I get that cash back, but then pay the balance before the month ends- to get to zero. This way, they don't charge me a high percentage rate of interest, or late fees. I am not being payed from Amazon to promote their credit card, just letting you know of a good deal that works for me. Shop around for your credit card and bank accounts. Do you really need to pay a yearly fee for your savings account? Likely you can find another provider without a fee. Some banks will give you a bonus check just for opening an account.

There are times when we buy things we don't have the money for- in that case, ask yourself if you need to buy that item. There is probably a better percentage rate out there so that you aren't just throwing interest rate money out the window. Larger purchases like a home or car would of course require a loan for most people, but shop around for the better interest rates. For college tuition and education costs, pay as much as you can up-front. Most colleges have payment plans for each semester that have zero interest. If you can do this, it's worth it. Think of it this way. You could pay $1000 per semester (for example) out of pocket in monthly payments. Or you could pay $2500 or more over the course of your repayment years, for the ability to not pay it back right away. If you have the money in the bank, use it wisely. Also, shop around for the best deal when it comes to your degree. You can usually find much less expensive options out there. If the top name school means a lot to you, ask yourself why that is.

If you are buried by debt, it can become impossible to dig yourself out. The longer you are in debt, the worse it becomes. Look for local organizations that help with this- there are solutions out there. I am not an expert in finances but my point is that we get used to living a certain type of lifestyle. Usually whatever amount of income we get used to, we find a way to spend it. When I was working my university job, I barely noticed a difference in my bank account savings when I got a raise (of almost double my salary). This was because I was already finding ways to spend that newly acquired money. It was funding an upcoming vacation, or a film project for example. I have more money saved now as a freelancer because I am more aware of my spending, and I am making an effort to save. Can you do the same?

Don't let yourself be fooled into thinking it's impossible to change your lifestyle. You can reduce your bills simply by getting rid of certain luxuries, or looking into alternatives. Maybe it's cutting out a certain shopping trip each week that was just cluttering up your home anyway. Or making handmade gifts for family rather than buying expensive items they will never use. Downsizing starts at home, and it can be as simple as having a yard sale or selling some of the junk in your closet that you forgot was there.

> *"When it comes to financial stability… you can make a reasonable budget. Obviously there's savings that comes into play as well. Even doing side jobs for a month or three months that will help you get that extra money that will help you do that trip you want to do. That will be time well spent because after three months, that's over and you can go on your journey. So, depending on what people are interested in doing there are various methods or ways to get to your goal. Creating a visual plan helps."*
> *–Magdalena Reilly: Documentary Filmmaker, Podcast Host, Minimalist & World Traveler*

However you need to work-out your expenses, go for it. This can be really difficult because people generally hate change. But you are creative, and you can do this. Think about what adds value to your life, and what bills or money sucking items/activities are in your life because you never questioned it. If it helps, think about how happy you will be when you have a life you love.

There are certainly many options for you, but it is up to you to decide what is best for your lifestyle. Freelancing doesn't always mean making less money. Here are some responses from successful freelancers with some tips on maximizing your income.

> *"If you are creative, have a clear vision and don't settle for less. You also need a good support network of mentors and friends and the biggest thing, that took me a while to learn was, never forget about cash flow! Even if it means having a small regular (but boring) income source of just a few hundred dollars on the side to cover rent and a bit of food. Just enough to keep stable but not enough that you get comfortable and stop hustling on the dream!"*
> *—Brett Solomano: Hollywood Stuntman, Author, Speaker and Coach*

> *"Definitely have a side-hustle or two, and scheduling is important. When you're juggling so many hats, make sure you actually allocate enough time so you're able to pursue your passion, and produce something of quality that you'll be proud of. On the other side of the spectrum, say you get consumed with pursuing your passion, make sure you make time to make ends meet."*
> *—Teraj: Actor, Model and Musician*

> *"Just like I'm constantly figuring out ways to create things, I'm constantly figuring out ways to make money doing art. I do lots of different things, like I'm starting to do tutorials and*

workshops. I put my stuff in some editorials, some are paid, some are not. Through my beginning years, I used to work for companies doing advertising photography for the bigger companies. That paid my bills for a while. Right now I'm opening a new studio... So it's another way just to be able to make money and put money into advertising. Trying to get bigger companies to use me as a freelance photographer. I'll start doing a lot more workshops, renting my studio out, then I do side jobs for my friends, headshots etc. So I'm all over the place trying to find ways to make money for my family."
–Michelle Engberg: Professional Photographer

When balancing multiple passions, the way I do with teaching and video, it can become difficult to know which opportunities to take and which to turn down. Some high paying temping or freelance gigs come along that look really tempting to me, but might not be the best for my lifestyle. Ultimately how I decide on these is based on the length of the assignment. If less than two months, I surely can take on a full time temp gig. If it is going to help my business grow, then absolutely yes I will do it. This is where I use my list of dealbreakers from the ideal career assessment. There are some things worth trying if it is going to help a larger cause, but you should have a set of standards that help guide you to make these decisions.

"During my time going back to school and in that in between time with the consulting firm that I had with my former business partner, I really wanted to learn... One of the wonderful things that she and I always said to one another was, 'whatever side job we were going to have while we tried to get our music business off the ground, it had to help the business in some way'. We didn't take any job that couldn't lend itself to a skillset that we were going to need. She went

off and worked for a social media company. She learned all about hashtags and all the different times to post and stuff like that. I wanted to learn about the contracts. That was really interesting to me. I became a paralegal and I learned a lot about contracts and what they should have in them and what all the different jargon meant and all that stuff. I got that job as I was in the midst of figuring out my business and going back to school. That was a good way to bring in money.

I think a lot of the times we feel as creatives, 'Oh, I'll just go be a waiter or waitress because that's flexible enough, it's what I need to do'. There's nothing wrong with that. There are definitely skill sets in the restaurant business that you can learn. I worked at Crate and Barrel as a merch manager. I was learning branding and all these different types of things and putting systems in place to make the best customer service possible. There's definitely things in there. But I think if we just take jobs for the sake of taking them and don't really try to be aware of what we can get out of them to help our dream job happen, then it's wasted time."
–Suzanne Paulinski: Mindset Coach for
Musicians & Industry Professionals

Everything you do and every assignment or gig you take should contribute towards your career, whether you are a freelancer or a full time employee. Always think about your resume. How is it going to look after this job, when you are searching again? It is okay to change your mind and shift gears. If you are sure about your skill set though and have a goal in mind, even if a job that comes along pays really well… is it worth sidetracking your career temporarily? If that money can be used to contribute to your ultimate goal, then the answer is yes. But make sure to give yourself a hard deadline on how long you will be there before you have enough money to leave and jump back onto your highway.

At the end of the day, it is just money. You have the power to make choices in your life. Money should not be the deciding factor when it comes to happiness or sadness. My husband and I used to have this argument for a long time until my persistence succeeded. He used to say that he was 'living for his weekends'. I can't even tell you how sad this used to make me. If we work five days a week at a job we hate, that means we're living for just roughly 28% of the days in our life. On top of that, most of us spend the latter half of Sunday night dreading our Monday morning return to work. I don't believe that is any way to live. Ideally we should be excited to go to a place where we spend most of our waking hours. If not excited, at least content or tolerant of it. There is no amount of money that can buy my happiness. I have seen the other side now that I have experimented with freelancing and gained clarity on my ideal career. Once you have a similar experience, you will never want to go back either:

> *"The bigger question is why am I doing what I'm doing? Why are we running around like this? For money? How much money do we want? When is it enough? What is it we get from money? What is underlying our pursuit of money? Is it safety, comfort, status, love, sense of belonging? If so, fair enough but can I give myself those things independent of the money? And then maybe the pursuit of money becomes a little more easy, and less tense, and there's not such a reliance on money. There's not such a heavy identification with whatever career prospects we set for ourselves. Then there's more creativity, and that sense of creativity is what really allows an artist to make amazing art. It's when they're freed up of that mental imprisonment. There are infinite creative possibilities to live and to live well, and there are people that demonstrate it. With or without*

money they create thriving, wholesome lives for themselves. A lot of people with a lot of money and they are devoid of life force, dry and lonely and sad- and they're some of the richest people I know. So money can't be the source."
-Anahita Moghaddam: Mindfulness
Coach & Speaker, Neural Beings

In this same podcast interview with Anahita, we discussed the cliche saying: "Do what you love and the money will come." That may be true, and I believe that, but she expands on this.

"Do what you do whether or not the money comes."
-Anahita Moghaddam: Mindfulness
Coach & Speaker, Neural Beings

Chase happiness, not money. Correction, embrace happiness. Because happiness is a choice we can make. If I'm in the moment, I can choose to be happy and hold onto that feeling. We can never hold on to money.

CHAPTER 10

Achieving Goals

After winning an Emmy award, I checked in with myself to assess how I felt after achieving this goal that had been on my list for so long. Surprisingly, I felt no different. It's normal to think that once we achieve our goals, we will feel more confident, satisfied, or that all our problems will go away. That was not the case for me. I felt exactly as confident and dissatisfied as I did before winning the Emmy. In fact, I was probably more dissatisfied because I realized that if I wanted to feel happy, I had to do something much bigger in my life than just win an award. Don't get me wrong, this award is very prestigious and it was difficult to win. I'm just saying that it was not the solution to my career issues. I felt capable of doing more, being more and contributing to a larger mission. I knew I didn't belong there and even worse, I felt that I had wasted time waiting around being comfortable when I really could have pushed myself to do something extraordinary. The problem was I didn't know where I wanted to go, let alone how to get there. It just didn't feel right.

Feelings are not logical all the time. They are not always measurable and not always accurate. For example, we might feel cranky and have a tendency to complain if we're hungry- I know I sure do. We learn about math, science, reading and other subjects in school, but no one ever teaches us how to listen to our feelings. This is probably because there is no scientific way to do so. It is unique for each person. I definitely can tell the difference between being hAngry (hungry+angry), and actually angry at someone for betraying me. These are different feelings both internally and externally, and for me, it originates in my gut and stomach. For you, discontendness might manifest as sweaty palms, a headache, heart racing, feeling scattered mentally or not able to concentrate. Whatever it is, realize your own patterns of physical stress, and learn to identify them over time. You are the master of you.

I like knowing I have the control to choose how I feel. For others, this may bring up feelings of anxiety. If so, like I would say for any piece of advice, if it doesn't work for you, try something else. It is all about our mindset and what can we tell ourselves to shift from negative to positive.

I'm not going to tell you to only focus on the positive. Identifying your happy place is just as important as identifying what you don't like. We SHOULD be paying attention and reflecting on what we dislike. When faced with a terrible job that you hate- what do you hate about it specifically? We did this in our past career assessment of positive and negatives, but I also encourage you to write as much as you can when you are going through a negative experience. This is because we tend to forget past details, and our memories may blend one experience with another. Not that you have to write every day in a journal, but do what you can to keep a record for yourself. This is important information especially when you have identified what it is that you absolutely hate about your current job or situation.

> "We don't reflect enough, at least that's what I've noticed with a lot of my clients. We're on this path and then we do it to the very bloody end and then we're like, 'Oh, did it work?' I think it's important to stop each week and be like, 'What's working so far? What's not working?' Because you don't know what you don't know until you know it. Each week, we're learning new things.

You have to constantly reassess your original plan."
-Suzanne Paulinski: Mindset Coach for
Musicians & Industry Professionals

Suzanne's book 'the Rock Star Life Planner' was really helpful for me in being able to understand what was happening to me during a very stressful time in my life. Once I was able to connect the feelings and overwhelmingly negative parts of that new job, with my past experiences, I was empowered to make the decision to freelance with confidence. Get specific about what you dislike and the reasons why. Look for patterns in your behavior to unlock your own personal triggers.

Is it the people at your job that make you hate it? If so, who specifically do you dislike? What is it about them that you dislike? Does that behavior or trait remind you of anyone else in your life? What lesson can you learn from dealing with this person, rather than fleeing the scene?

Use the situation you are currently in to identify and eventually eliminate your own personal triggers. I urge you to think about how you have contributed to this unhealthy relationship, and if you can, work on fixing it before you move on so that you can maintain the relationship. The importance of networking is huge in today's competitive job-market. If you do not have to leave on bad terms, don't. You never know who you might have to call on in a time of need.

There is always a reason to make amends with someone, except when there isn't. If they are malicious, mean-spirited or are actively trying to harm you- that is not a relationship worth saving. That is up to you to decide, and having a conversation about our intentions is usually a good way to find out the truth from someone.

What if we like the people we work with (or are indifferent towards them), but it's a specific task in our job that we hate? If these things we don't like are something that can be avoided or delegated to someone else without issue, then do that. If it is something we must do, then make a game-plan for how you are going to tackle this task in small chunks. I also suggest taking a class or workshop that can help you make this task more enjoyable. Usually we dislike certain tasks because we are not good at it- this is an unnecessary self-judgement. For me, I used to dislike writing descriptions for my podcast because I felt like they are not as good as other people's descriptions, and because it takes me (what I believe to be) a long time to complete. My game-plan could either be to take a class in writing, or to delegate this task to someone else. It is important to note that when delegating you MUST give up control. You must accept that whomever is now doing this task will have creative control over it, and that their success is measured only by how well you have communicated the task to them, and how you encourage them to get better at it.

Delegating is not for everyone and it requires a lot of patience. I have delegated my podcast description writing to two different companies, neither of whom successfully achieved what I would call success. I had to rewrite the descriptions, which took much longer than it would have taken for me to just do it myself. At first I was getting emotional about their lack of care for the task. I felt that they were not putting in the effort that was required to write a good description. That was extremely frustrating, especially when I was paying them good money to do this work. No one is going to have as much care for something that belongs to you, as you would have for it. If it is something that is important to you, you might want to do it yourself. Otherwise we have to start trusting others to do it, but know that it will not be the same (could be better or worse). The success of that task is based on how well you communicate your needs, and the interpretation and skill level of the person you are delegating it to.

In some jobs, we are not in a position to delegate work, or we do not have control over the outcome. In these situations I would suggest assessing whether or not this task is something we will have to do again in the future. Using my podcast description example, even if I stop doing my podcast, I will always have to learn how to write short, catchy descriptions that will get people to read my book or watch my videos. So my decision would be to stop avoiding it, and just get better at it! Or to find someone that I really trust, and train them to write all of my descriptions/blurbs for me (however expensive this may be). However, when relying on others, even if we train someone to our own satisfaction, we do not own that person and cannot control their willingness to do the task. Learning how to get better at writing (for me) would be a win-win because I would become faster at it, and it gives me the knowledge to be able to teach this task to others- increasing the success rate for whomever I hire.

This is an example of a task that is stressful for me, but not necessarily for everyone. Remember that stress is part of any job. We are after all, making money in exchange for goods or services. Stress is a common occurrence for anyone whether you are working or not. I'm not asking you to eliminate stress, or assume there is a job out there that has no stress at all. I am asking you to measure how much of that stress is necessary, and how much is too much to where you might start to have health issues or otherwise be shortening the length of or decreasing the value of your life. Remember that when you are choosing your career path, it is not just about work. You have to incorporate lifestyle choices and what works best for you personally, physically and emotionally. We are human beings not machines.

Also, learn how to discern stress versus a feeling of dissatisfaction versus boredom. It may not be logical and you might not be able to measure it, but it is important to discern one from the other. For example, as a freelancer today I have moments where I am working by myself and feeling very unsure at times. This is a normal feeling to have, and I can get past it by taking a moment to breathe and look for a rational solution. Or perhaps I have to reach out to someone who can help or provide advice. Whatever it is, this stress is a normal part of freelancing. Then there is the stress of your boss yelling at you, abusing you mentally or physically, or even the stress of having a micro-manager who takes credit for your work, but throws you under the bus whenever there isn't a favorable opinion of the final product. I digress. There are different degrees of stress, and you have to know your own personal boiling point.

If you are dealing with stress that harms you physically or emotionally, it's time to go. If your job doesn't challenge you, but you want to grow, I would advise looking for ways to grow outside of the job. Or maybe you can inquire about possibilities to take on more responsibility, or transfer to a different department. Think outside the box and don't be fooled into thinking there are only choices A or B. Truth is there are endless possibilities and YOU get to decide how you design your life and career.

Before you quit your job that you hate, go back to your Past Career Assessment. Look at everything you wrote in the negative column for this current job. Do any of these repeat from the past? For the ones that overlap, ask yourself why they are issues for you. Perhaps this is something that you have an issue with in your personal life as well. Don't be afraid to dig deep emotionally. If it is something new, just look out for this when applying to new jobs. There is definitely an emotional side to your decisions. Don't let your emotions completely freeze you in fear, but listen to them for clues. The better you get at listening to your gut, the better you are at turning off the emotions that are not helpful.

"Trust in my process, trust in my destiny that something is about to happen but I have to build my character to prepare myself for it. Because for everything in the future there will be joys but there will always be challenges. It's good to face the challenges now because greater challenges await us. Successful people have to face challenges so this is a training

ground. How to strengthen our hearts, develop steel courage,
find peace and calm and to believe that things will be better."
-Alma-Villegas Schwalbenberg, PHD

I know, you're looking for validation and permission to quit your job today. So far, I have only given possible suggestions for solutions to make the job work. That isn't completely true. If you plan on staying in a similar role or field after you quit your job, it will be beneficial to learn new skills, get better at tasks you dislike, and to maintain your network. Learning how to listen to your gut, and overcome stress will be helpful in any situation. It is important to realize that no job and no career will be perfect.

CHAPTER 11

ASK FOR WHAT YOU WANT

If you are absolutely convinced that you have to leave your current job, there is no better time than now. It is amazing what we can accomplish in a few weeks. Give yourself a short deadline to make the connections you need, and stick to it. Don't be fooled into thinking you have to wait until you have a certain amount of money in the bank, or something else lined up. A lot of time can be lost this way. As discussed, savings can be a helpful tool before going freelance. Perhaps if you don't have savings, there might be a temp assignment that is a better transition for you.

Instead of staying stagnant out of fear, start reaching out to local organizations, businesses and the people you know (before you make the jump). Tell them what you are looking for ideally, based on that positives list. If they don't know of anything, maybe they can keep you in mind for future opportunities, or pass along your resume to someone who can help. Don't be afraid to reach out to your network, no matter how big or small. The key here is to be clear on what you are looking for, and not just regurgitate your resume from what you are currently doing, or have done in the past. Let them know what you ideally see yourself doing and why your past experience gives you the ability to achieve these tasks. For example, I didn't have any experience teaching kids, aside from one summer as a camp counselor back in high school. Even that job was not exactly "teaching." When I decided that I wanted to teach though, I wrote a resume that focused every job experience's bullet points on the teaching aspect. For my university job listing, I summarized all the video production tasks into one bullet point. Then put the second bullet point as all my teaching duties where I trained others, gave presentations or coached junior producers on-set. Remember that each type of job requires a new resume, and don't be afraid to have multiple versions for yourself.

> *"Know your worth. Be confident that THAT is your worth. And don't apologize or question it. Simply explain, factually, why you're worth it."*
> *–Diana Cherkas: Freelance Actor, Writer,*
> *Advertising Copywriter & Copy Editor*

Only you can decide when it is the right time to make a change. For me, I don't feel like I had a choice. The new job I took on was not good for my health. I only stayed for a month. I knew that I wouldn't have enough time to find a new full time job before I quit, so I embraced the idea that I would be a freelancer, and I asked for what I wanted. Keeping my lifestyle preferences in mind, I focused on local places I could drive to, or easily commute to by train. Also, I set my freelance rate higher than my normal full time rate, and I let potential employers know that I preferred a part time schedule. This is how I created my own career plan, rather than just choosing from the jobs posted online.

Think about it, any time an employer posts a job, they are asking for a specific set of skills and experiences- an ideal employee. Why shouldn't we have that same power? We know what we want, what we are good at and the ideal lifestyle we want to live. Rather than just applying to jobs that somewhat fit that description, we should be reaching out and asking for exactly what we want. Sometimes we will send an email or make a call, and get no response, but the likelihood of this is the same as if we are applying to a job posting online.

The same principle applies when we are in a job interview. It only hurts us to be quiet and not ask questions. An interview is a two-way conversation. We should be asking for what we want, and asking questions that tell us whether this job is right for us. Take the stress out of interviewing and walk in there confident that you are going to have a conversation with someone else that will determine whether this opportunity is best for all parties. If we are being specific and asking for what we want, we are more likely to get it. At the very least, by asking questions, we can avoid situations that are similar to our past negatives. We can sniff out the deal breakers by asking questions.

When finding your ideal next move, use that list you made, and be open to new possibilities. Use your past experiences, and the interests you had as a child to guide you to your ideal future career. No dream is too big or small. It is possible to have a career that you love. Be open to the various forms of that ideal career, and know that you can create it for yourself. There is no cookie cutter job that works for everyone. It takes trial, error and your own self-analysis to choose your next move. Remember that freelance versus full time is just a detail, just like a salary, or a job title. Don't get attached to that. Instead, follow your WHY and use your lifestyle choices to identify the big picture.

Remember the flow tasks from your ideal career assessment list? Your ideal career should have a mix of these plus new challenges and opportunities for you to explore. Whenever I have a camera in my hand, I am extremely focused and lose sense of time. I get so lost that I have no worries or concerns of previous stress that might have been going on. This has been the case since I was in high school, and I have the same feeling when filming a video. When I started learning about video production, I realized that my other skills came into play as well. There is organization, leadership and problem solving involved. This is a great field for me because I can utilize my inherent and learned skills, and I look forward to the extremely creative and stress-reducing flow task of photography. You can combine your multiple skills and interests into your chosen career.

> "[My job] It's like a therapy session. Instead of paying $300, you are able to get it out in your art. I was very unhappy doing anything else with my life. I did tons of jobs, managed a moving company, a receptionist and for some reason I was always unhappy. I couldn't find that outlet. I realized that when you're meant to be an artist, that's what you've got to do. It's a lot of sacrifice and a lot of hard times because it's very competitive, the world out there, but you have to be happy doing what you do in your life."
> –Michelle Engberg: Professional Photographer

> "You go [to concerts for free] and you get to be so close to the artists. Sometimes you get to interview them if there's time and if there's an offer. So you get to meet these people and it's just really, really fun. It's an experience."
> –Mayra Ramales: Founder &
> Manager of theSoundLive.com

Form versus function is important when choosing your next step. We can think that we want to do one thing, but then learn it's not for us. That is totally okay. This is what I learned when I took journalism, and found out that I prefer visual storytelling to writing articles. In this example, the function is journalism, the forms were video versus writing articles. It happened again when I got into teaching (function) and learned that I prefer to teach older kids rather than the little ones (form). It's about the details. The more you immerse yourself into different experiences, the more you can refine your goals and what works best for you. This is why we wrote that list out. You will see similar functions, but realize that the different forms are where you had an emotional connection or discontentment.

Michelle Engberg explains in her podcast episode that she first enrolled in classes for video production, but this lead her to her current career, photography.

> *"What I realized in photography is that it could be just a one man show and you can create one picture to tell a whole story. That really appealed to me and I wondered how can I do that and really push the boundaries of photography. I was always trying to push myself even harder to get better."*
> *–Michelle Engberg: Professional Photographer*

This is an example of form versus function. She kept in mind her personality preferences and lifestyle choices, and that lead her to photography. Since photography and video production use a lot of the same skills, she was able to transfer that knowledge.

Don't underestimate the power of your past experience, and what you do every day successfully. Try thinking of a different way to use these skills that you have. For example, I love interviewing people, and was doing this in the video production process (but not often enough). So, I started a podcast to combine that passion for interviewing with my curiosity for the creative process. Now, I am re-using that content to create this book. Writing this book is a new challenge for me, and I am making the process easier by incorporating something I am comfortable and familiar with.

> *"You bring with you whatever experience you have from other jobs or other things in life… and don't underestimate*

the experience you've had as a producer if you want to become an editor. Or whatever experience you've had in life. It will probably help you be better at whatever it is you want to do."
—Janis Vogel: Professional TV & Film Editor

"Over these last two and a half, almost three years, I've been working with clients to get them better organized. To get them prioritizing their tasks a little bit better. I kept creating all these different templates for them. At the beginning of this year, I just thought to myself, I have all these templates collected that I've created over the years, and they lend themselves well to a planner. I remember last December looking for hours at Barnes & Noble's for a planner that really suited my needs. Because there's a creative person that has their own business, we have social media to worry about and worrying about our finances each week and what we're bringing in, all these different things. I wanted to combine the templates I created that included tracking inventory and keeping track of your social media contacts, all of those things. I decided to put them in a book. A good friend of mine from back at my days at Drexel helped me design it and make it look pretty. It was a really fun project for us to work on together."
—Suzanne Paulinski: Mindset Coach for
Musicians & Industry Professionals

"All those skills that I have from business school, I am using them now because running a private practice requires a lot of decision making and business knowledge. You have to know how to manage your practice... It's a process. I wish things could kind of just settle and be like that. I find that my life has moving pieces all the time

and I like that. I like the challenge. Running a private practice is challenging and I'm growing as an individual and a therapist. I'm growing as a business owner as well because there are opportunities to learn and there are new things I can always apply to the work I do. I'm always in search of new ideas and how I can improve my business."
-Arta Cakaj, MS, LCAT: Wholehearted Art Therapy

Dip your toe in the water by trying part time gigs or freelance opportunities, before you commit. Do you research to find out how much money you can make from these gigs, so you can price your services accordingly? You might need to pick up new skills or add something to your repertoire so that you can make sure you are bringing in a reasonable income. Our imagination is helpful here, but not always accurate. Try out as many different gigs as you can and see what works for you.

It definitely is not good in the eyes of a recruiter, to have a bunch of short term jobs on your resume, if you plan on going back to full time work eventually. If they are part time or part of a freelance period, that can be easily explained. A resume is an important thing. However, finding your path is the number one priority, which is why I suggest doing part time or freelance gigs. It maintains your resume integrity without it seeming like you were just unemployed for a number of months, or jumped from job to job without care.

"I was always very creative, and I needed to find outlets for me to put my creativity into. It's not until I found visual outlets that I was really able to express myself fully. I was able to learn things a lot easier. For me when I was younger, struggling to find my path as an artist. I was jumping into different things and trying to learn what is my passion and what I really loved in the art field whether it be drawing or music. Those were all just outlets for me to eventually become a

photographer and finally find my path after a million years."
–Michelle Engberg: Professional Photographer

"I kind of fell into [freelancing]. I left my agency of four years in San Francisco to relocate to San Diego. Had a full time interview straight out the gate and it was between me and one other candidate. The other candidate inched me out and since I had been marketing myself as a freelancer, the work started rolling in. Since then, I've been working fairly consistently over the last two years or so and it's been working out great. Would I take a full time position? Probably, but it would have to check all of the boxes and I would likely ask for a three to six month contract to test the new company out to ensure it was a good fit before signing on full time."
–Bryant Coffey: Freelancer in
the Advertising Industry

"When I was at LaGuardia Community College, I was in this special program called ASAP. They were starting this journalism program and a newspaper. They wanted students to pitch ideas. I always wanted to do a music blog or a music site on any website that would give me the time of day. I approached the director who was in charge of that... he said he does concert photography, that we'll talk after. I just kept in touch with him, and I shared my dreams- that since I was little I wanted to do music journalism and work for a magazine or something. He offered to get me something, and he had a friend at NextMosh.com. He gave me a shot, and his other friend who runs Tri-State Indie too... I just submitted and sent them some shows I wanted to cover and I got in. That's how I started doing it.

At first it was a trial, but then they liked it, and so I stayed for about eight months. Throughout that time, I really appreciated them letting me build my portfolio and get the experience. After that I realized that I wanted my own thing... I want to be my own boss."
*   -Mayra Ramales: Founder &*
*   Manager of theSoundLive.com*

Doing what you love is a risk, but it is also risky to waste time in your life doing something you don't love. Remember that you have to ask for what you want, and be confident in who you are. Each person has their own unique combination of skills. If you can identify those unique talents, you can get started testing out the ways you can use them to have your ideal career. It takes a lot of hard work, but it should feel like an enjoyable process because you are doing what is best for you. You are being your authentic self.

"You gotta get on stage all the time, as much as you can. Sometimes it's just annoying because you might have to do the open mic with that one drunk guy, you might have to do the dungeon show. But the more you get up, the more confident you become with your material. You have to get to a place where you feel comfortable being yourself. Being yourself is the only thing that's gonna make you different. We live in a society where everyone is encouraging you to be like somebody else. But then if you're like everybody else how are you gonna stand out? You're not unique anymore."
*   -Angela Star: Comedian*

"I tried to be open to all experiences, and I tried to be flexible... I learned that we want to take charge of our life but we also have to be aware that things happen through

us and a big part is also the opportunities that is offered to us. So, I just made time in my life to regularly check where I am at that point in time. So that's how I made some drastic decisions. I decided to quit my job- I could have waited to be laid off and people were asking me why are you quitting when people are losing their job. We follow what the gut, the inner spirit says and when you jump you make the leap of faith and everything falls into place."
                                       -Alma-Villegas Schwalbenberg, PHD

"From a financial point of view especially if it's something that you're passionate about you just have to find a way to make ends meet. For me, my livelihood doesn't come from music yet. Although it's my full time job at this point, I'm still surviving off of my modeling gigs, real estate, etc. So, I think it's important if you're going into something like the entertainment industry that you have something else going on at the same time, just so you can be able to survive."
                                       -Teraj: Actor, Model and Musician

"Especially because you have a whole family and kids and bills and a house. To decide that I'm gonna be an artist now, and if we don't make money and if we live in a box on the street, it's okay. We'll figure it out."
                                       -Michelle Engberg: Professional Photographer

You have to have faith in the universe, and in yourself that you will do whatever it takes to make the best out of any situation. You will find ways to make money even if it means working multiple jobs, long hours, or giving up your current way of life. When I quit my full time job, I was terrified, but I knew that the work I had put in during the past few years would help me. I knew I would do whatever it takes to survive and succeed. Even though freelancing might not be my long-term goal, it is wonderful to know that it is an option that I can make work if need be.

Having faith should not stop us from making effort towards our goals, or pushing past our comfort zone. We should be aware of the signs we see around us, and open to the opportunities that just pop up seemingly out of nowhere. Sometimes they are unexpected, and feel like the timing is completely wrong. It is up to you to decide which opportunities you say yes to, but I believe that if something is presented to us, there has to be a reason. Either we are supposed to learn the lesson of how to say NO to this thing we no longer want to do, or we have to jump faithfully into this new adventure. I have been offered jobs very similar to the last job that I quit. I said no confidently because I am clear on what I do NOT want. This is John Trigonis' email response to me after I asked him how he was able to land the ideal job (for him) of working at Indiegogo.

"I wasn't actually looking for a job, and that's how I found one, or one found me five years ago. My philosophy is that if you put in your time, energy, and effort into your passions, someone will take notice. In my case, that's exactly what happened. I spent ten years making short films, going to some festivals, making more short films, and then stumbled on crowdfunding. I did that as creatively as I would any of my films, and it jump started me into a world of consultations, book-writing, and eventually Indiegogo took notice of me and brought me onto their team. A lot of this was being in the right place at the right time.

I do my job well not because I'm a strategist, but because I can think creatively about solutions that would elude even the most seasoned of strategists out there who paint-by-numbers, rinse and repeat, simply because they are not creators themselves.

In truth, I'm fortunate to count myself among those who do love their day job, but any job, no matter how much one loves it, is not the measure of a good life, but rather the means to an easier one."
—John T. Trigonis: Filmmaker, Poet & Indiegogo's Head Film and Creative Campaign Strategist

CHAPTER 12

LIVE TO WORK, OR WORK TO LIVE?

If having a job we love will make our lives easier, then we have to redefine our definition of easy. A lot of us believe that easy means we are lazy, or not working hard. That is simply untrue. I have heard from a number of motivational gurus explaining that when you are doing what you love, it will come easy. Everything will fall into place without having to push so hard. If we are resisting, then certainly something must be wrong. It must not be meant to be, or perhaps we are not ready for it. I believe all of this to a certain extent.

We have to work hard to make a change in our life. Doing something we hate can be just as easy as fighting for something we love. In previous chapters so far you have read my experience and that of others who have had high-paying jobs with great benefits. Maybe we had easy jobs that didn't challenge us at all, yet we gave that up for something that seems more difficult. Here is where the distinction between easy and lazy comes in. If we are just taking the money from a job we absolutely hate and we know is not right for us, we are being lazy. We know we can do more, contribute to the greater good, be better and do better- yet we would rather take the easy route. There is nothing wrong with being lazy. Some people believe that money is just the means to live the life you want. However, life is short. We spend a lot of time working. Why not increase the value of your life by making your career something that fulfills you?

Easy on the other hand, comes into play when we speak about flow. Flow happens when we are working on tasks that make time go faster. Tasks that we are perfectly content with doing, and our brain goes on autopilot because we are just in the moment. Flow is ease, not laziness. Ease, in the bigger picture, is taking on opportunities that come to us, rather than chasing things that others have. For example, I was fighting my teaching bug for a long time, thinking that all I want to do is create high-level TV shows and feature films. I saw the people who were successfully working in Hollywood and I was chasing the illusion of whatever they had, even though it wasn't right for my lifestyle.

There is no guarantee that working in Hollywood would make me any more money than I make now, and that was proven to me when I met a good number of production assistants who work 12 hour days for $10 per hour. Money aside, I was chasing fame, awards, and status. It was my ego taking control. Chasing this was not easy or lazy at all. I was going to networking events and panel discussions, kissing butts and feeling like I was not as good as the people who were working in this industry. When I won my Emmy award, it's as if my brain snapped out of it. I didn't care anymore about stature or awards. I started focusing on what people often ask me for- training, advice, and education. It was so much easier to put myself out there as a teacher, and to learn these new skills. It's as if I already had some of the knowledge within me, all along. Each teaching experience gives me insight into something new about myself. It is a cycle of growth. It feels right.

Just a few years later I would consider myself as 50% teacher, and 50% content creator. I have the flow in my content creation tasks, but as a teacher I am constantly learning and growing. This is ease, and more importantly, balance. The teaching experiences I have fill me with a sense of purpose, and they make me feel like what I'm doing has a positive impact on others. It's not a competition for who has the biggest ego, who has worked on the most prestigious projects or who can name-drop better. Not that there's anything wrong with that industry and the people who work in it. If you want to live an easy life, you have to find what is easy for your lifestyle and unique personality, with just the right amount of challenge and growth for YOU.

> *"I fell in love with editing then but I never saw it as a career path. I was afraid of it in some ways. Sometimes the technical pressure seemed daunting. Then sometimes I was like, 'This is too fun, I can't do this for money. This is a passion.' I didn't really know whether I was good at it. I just like doing it. It became a no-brainer when I was later making music videos and things like that. I'm enjoying the technical aspects of this. I'm enjoying the creative aspects. I'm able to be myself. It just worked."*
> *-Janis Vogel: Professional TV & Film Editor*

> *"I feel like the kids give me material in my own life. They have no filter and sometimes being a comedian you fall under the pressures of being like everyone. I'm teaching them how to be themselves and they're teaching me how to be myself. I love it. They come in and say the funniest thing and that kind of triggers a joke for me in my own life. Just working with them is so funny, laugh after laugh. I love it."*
> *-Angela Star: Comedian*

If we are being lazy, like I used to be, we would wait around for the job we currently have to give us opportunities to grow. This is the same job we know is not right for us, that hasn't challenged us the entire time. The job that doesn't have our personal interest in mind.

It is lazy to sit around hoping that you can change something that will not change. When you know what you want to do, it is more likely to happen if we put the work in and create it for ourselves. In the short term this is hard to do. In the long run though, we are setting ourselves up for success because we are defining our own potential.

"To anyone who wants to start doing it [journalism or photography], just create your own outlet. Nowadays with technology- everyone looks down on it [a website] because people say it's not credible journalism. These are people who have graduated with a journalism degree [many years ago]. I think you need to forget about that and really… if you want to do it, don't wait for someone to give you that opportunity. You could go ahead and do it yourself. Start local in whatever field it is that you want to pursue. Start local and with time you will grow. You just have to keep on going. Don't be limited. Don't feel like you have to wait for someone to open that door for you because you can just create it yourself."
–Mayra Ramales: Founder &
Manager of theSoundLive.com

"I really think that it's a heart driven thing. When your heart is calling for you to do something, you have no idea why. Even if it seems crazy, I always think, "Why not?" Instead of thinking why, why not."
–Julia Amisano: Singing, Piano & Acting Teacher

"Start small and build something. Always be selling. Always be pitching. If you aren't making money from what you're doing now and want to, just try and make your first $10 and go up from there. If you have an idea, make sure you can build it. The world is full of dreamers who never followed through."
-Brett Solomano: Hollywood Stuntman,
Author, Speaker and Coach

"I am still learning as I go, so there's never a day where I feel that I know everything. You have to grow and adjust and do your best."
-Barbara Saint Aimé, Publicist (Aimé Agency)

"[Starting my own business] wasn't super easy in the beginning. You have to be more organized than you've ever been before. I promise that because I'm also a mom, I'm a wife, I was a student when I first started. So, I had a lot to juggle. The way that I was able to get this done was that I had my 9-to-5 with an hour lunch. On my hour lunch, I was somewhere reading, researching, drafting an email or working on graphics and communication. I didn't outsource, I did everything 100% myself. I was also working on my book. I ended up using my lunch break every single day that I was at work. When I left work, I came home and after I had my son ready for bed, there I was again at minimum 90 minutes a day Monday through Friday working on something, anything related to my business. As it began to progress I was able to join mastermind groups online. I spent my weekends at different events, networking. So, all the free time that we take for granted, use that free time to build your business. You're already giving your employer 40

or more hours a week. You need to make sure you're giving your business enough time, even if it's an hour or two a day to help build that. Giving it 15 minutes here or there on Instagram is not going to be enough to build your business."
-Temica Gross: Budget Business Coach

"I work as a receptionist so when the phones were slow I would write, or look up something, but still work. I don't like to have the two interfere with one another. It was hard. I was just trying to juggle it. So, I basically was working seven days a week because on the weekends I was doing location scouting, doing casting calls. It was a lot of that."
-Gabrielle Aliké Hawkins: Filmmaker

Let's say that what you are aspiring to is a new skill or field of work. The transition is not easy. There is a lot of overlapping time where you are juggling multiple jobs and working a lot of extra hours. The other difficulty is learning something new. There are tests, papers to write, practice to hone your craft, trial and error. The trick is to see if you enjoy learning about this new thing. You should get a true sense of enjoyment or fulfillment from learning about this new subject. If you enjoy it, that is definitely easier than learning something you hate. That time will go by faster and you won't feel like you're working. You will know the difference immediately.

"If you love to learn, then you can learn anything. If you fall in love with the process of learning, struggling and figuring things out than you can learn whatever it is that you're supposed to do."
-Mayra Ramales: Founder &
Manager of theSoundLive.com

"I actually taught myself photography. I started in 2010 just learning how to use my camera and everything was pretty much self-taught. Then I started getting good enough where I could get clients and get jobs through other companies. That built my skill up a lot more to where I could start shooting advertising and commercial work for bigger brands. When you really love something and you spend a lot of time doing it, you end up learning quite quickly. Now with the internet, and YouTube is amazing with their tutorials so I just kept practicing and learned it real quick."
-Michelle Engberg, Professional Photographer

"Journalism is ever-changing... There really are no rules. Especially now with all of this technology. I've been doing this since I was 18, straight out of high school. I never took any journalism classes, it was just go out there and learn. You can't put any limitations on what you do. You learn through the process."
-Mayra Ramales: Founder &
Manager of theSoundLive.com

"I think it's important to continue learning all the time. I think it's also important to make sure that the industry provides ways for people to learn. As you know, I run an organization called the Blue Collar Post Collective. We have that goal in mind, to provide educational experiences as well as all the other things we do for our members.

Education is huge. Whether we are posting educational stuff on our Facebook or doing workshops... Luckily, you can join that for free. That's the great thing

about us, and finding other free ways to learn. I've got my first assistant editor job on the show, 'Teen Mom 2'. I learned Avid in two weeks on Lynda.com."
-Janis Vogel: Professional TV & Film Editor

You certainly don't have to enroll in an accredited school or accrue student loan debt in order to learn something new and take on a new career path. There are so many resources on the internet today and even free in your community that you can take advantage of. Maybe a fellowship or internship is right for you, because you just need a bit of hands-on training and to make some connections. If you're in the video or photography industry, check your local public access station or community center for training. Look for meetups in your community, free classes or one on one tutoring.

Do not underestimate the power of conferences and online publications related to your niche. That could be a magazine, influencer or expert that you subscribe to in the mail, digitally, or follow on social media for the latest news. It is really important, especially in fields that are technology-driven, to keep up with the latest advances and changes. This will give you small talk for your interviews and networking events. It will also give you important information about what you should be learning, so you can stand out from your competition and not get left behind.

Perhaps your current job offers free training that could help you reach your personal goals. If so, take advantage of that. If that day job does not offer any opportunities to learn, don't let that stop you. Create a project for yourself that explores whatever it is you want to learn. For example, my podcast interviews are a way to learn from experienced professionals. This podcast platform is also proof that I can execute and share the episodes with an audience. So when I reach out to a famous Ted Talk speaker, author, or actress asking them to be a guest, I am less likely to get ignored. I am showing them proof of what I can do for them. More importantly, they are going to teach me what I want to learn, and I get to have a casual conversation with a stranger, who later becomes a friend. Squeaky Moore used a similar strategy to her advantage. When writing her book, "The Pitch 101," she was able to get one on one interviews with industry experts. This was because she approached them not as wanting to pitch them an idea, but wanting to feature them in her book. Learning can be facilitated in many ways. You don't have to wait for a reason to learn. If there is something you are curious about, find a way to educate yourself. Be open to all possibilities to learn.

> *"When I started building my business I went straight in with communications and graphic design, built my own web pages, email platforms- everything I did it on my own. I didn't know how well I could do it until I actually tried. With this information that I have as it relates to my personal life, I took this back to my corporate job and showed them what I was capable of doing outside of my job. I ended up landing a role on the national communications team for our company. This was the best thing ever because I'm here working in a national communications role and they're teaching me different sorts of platforms. I was anti-Wordpress for a long time but here I am with all this Wordpress training, paid for by the company because I was able to convince them that I knew what I was doing. I was able to mirror what I was doing both corporate and private for my business. I know it's not ideal for everyone to be able to do that, but if you can, figure out how to take what you're doing in your personal life with your business and bring it over to the corporate side of wherever you're working. It will only help you and make your personal business that much stronger by getting that free training from your company."*
> *-Temica Gross: Budget Business Coach*

"[My book] is about being able to learn anything. I think often people go through school and expect to come out on the other end with one degree, one certificate, one qualification. Then they're like 'cool, now I've got this path built for me' supposedly they're thinking. 'And after university I'm gonna get a job and be set for life'. Nobody says that but I think everyone believes it. Me, even since I've been here in the US, I've had 20-30 different companies that I've worked for already. I don't know how many I've had in Australia but it's definitely hundreds in total. I've got over 30 different qualifications and for me, that really just colors my experience, just being able to say yes to everything, being a bit of an opportunist. If something comes to me, 'do I want to take this right now? Seems like fun. Let's do that'. I never have to say that I'll just watch. I can really step into it, whether it's an experience with friends or a job, I can always step into it and take it on. That's what the book is about. It's ten different strategies that I've used to be able to step into my life."
—Brett Solomano: Hollywood Stuntman,
Author, Speaker and Coach

"In my experience, the key to being a successful freelancer is adaptability. I started out as a programmer. I was working, and not happy, and ended up in an office next to some copy editors who all loved their jobs. So I pivoted. I took a class, got my foot in the door, and loved it. An actor colleague reached out about doing voiceover work, asking if I could record from home. This wasn't an audition, it was an offer of work. I said yes, and set up a basic home studio with a borrowed mic. A year later, I'm still recording regularly. I've upgraded my studio accordingly, and just added a new voiceover client last week. If something

sounds appealing, figure out how to do it. Picking up a new skill or pivoting into a new industry with your existing skill will only make you more appealing in the long run."
–Diana Cherkas: Freelance Actor, Writer,
Advertising Copywriter & Copy Editor

You can always grow and improve. Don't let your lack of knowledge or resources stop you from trying something new. If you love learning, your potential is limitless.

CHAPTER 13

THE TRIFECTA

I have this theory called the TRIFECTA. It says that each of us have three tasks or roles we should be doing, to create our ideal career. The variety from these three different roles will keep us excited, always learning, financially stable and fulfilled. It's like diversifying your income stream, where the income is not just money but overall abundance. To come up with your own trifecta, let's start with the three essential ingredients for a good life: *Happiness, Love & Success*.

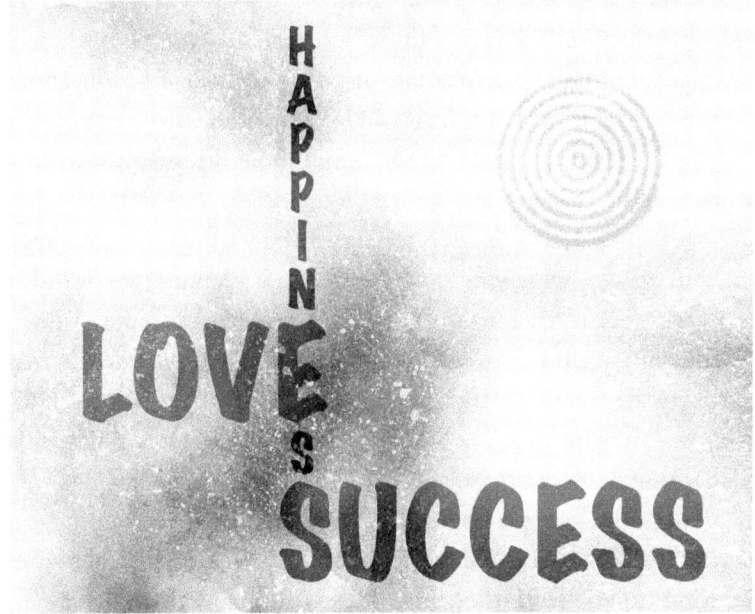

This trifecta for a good life serves as a guide to any new opportunity that I take on. Does this new opportunity contribute to any or all of these three qualities? If not, can I modify this opportunity to fit my ideal lifestyle? Can I leave room for a hobby that will help me achieve all of these?

Using this formula, think of three aspects of your career that contribute to these three qualities. They don't all have to work for each one. My career trifecta is Film + Teaching + Art. It could also be phrased as Media + Education + Art. The terminology doesn't matter because I know what each of these words signifies to me. I use the addition sign because they all are tied together for a greater purpose.

Film/Media has brought me success for over ten years. I am very experienced in this field and I achieve flow most easily when working on videos. Teaching fills me with love, a sense of wanting to give back, and helps me be a better person. Meanwhile, education is a life-long journey for me and I want to continue learning forever.

I make most of my freelance income from teaching and film/video production. The two of those things are tied together where I often teach filmmaking, or make films that are related to education. I am pursuing a Master's degree in learning and educational technology that will tie these together even more. Film and teaching work together for me, and generally define my career. If you can tie together two parts of your trifecta (or more), then you are surely on your way to living your best life. Can you identify two or three aspects of your trifecta that make you money, and contribute to flow?

The third factor, Art, is a larger idea that I use to define my curiosity for creativity, and the unpaid activities that I do such as painting, drawing, and reading about art history. Art is essentially something I do for myself as a way to unwind. Art brings me happiness- it is simple as that. I rarely make money from my art because I like to have full creative control over it. This makes it a relaxing experience rather than a stress-inducing one. Not every project has to be something we share or use for financial profit. When we don't worry about marketing, or selling, or staying within certain parameters for a client, we activate a different part of our brain.

"I'm a poet mostly and I always wrote poetry because it was short. I could finish it in a day. I could present it or get it published or whatever by the next following week. It was very quick and easy. I always like those quick and easy things."
-John T. Trigonis: Filmmaker, Poet & Indiegogo's
Head Film and Creative Campaign Strategist

Art is my form of play and it sparks my creativity. I find that having a creative hobby that is a departure from my normal medium, is helpful in getting that juices flowing in other areas. We do the same thing over and over again for our job, so it's nice to shift this routine to try something completely different. For me, I am using my hands to paint, getting dirty, moving around as music plays. I don't do this all the time but when I do, I feel really free. It gives me ideas for videos and clarity in whatever else I'm working on. I'm taking my attention away from a certain work project and somehow painting helps me focus even more and gain clarity on that project. After taking a step away from whatever else I'm working on, I come back reinvigorated. I keep art just for me. It is okay to keep one part of your trifecta unrelated to your career or income-stream. Do what works best for you. Have you identified a third aspect of your trifecta yet?

"I've told a lot of musicians, 'Maybe you don't want to make this a career'. Just because you love what you do doesn't necessarily mean that that should be the way you make money because it is a job, it is work and it is sacrifice and compromise in order to make that happen. If there's

something that's so sacred to you that you don't want to compromise it for anything, then 100% I'd say, keep it a hobby and keep it your side passion that feeds you and only you. Maybe you share your art with other people or maybe you do a free gallery night or something like that, but without the pressure of needing to make it something or having any expectations of it. Yes, I think that's so important to keep certain things like that sacred. Unfortunately, just the sheer word 'commercial', it comes with a price. I think that's wonderful advice to keep a side passion that's just yours."
—Suzanne Paulinski: Mindset Coach for
Musicians & Industry Professionals

"I also started doing fine art pieces which I'm hoping to get into galleries. I started my fine art stuff probably in 2011. That I love a lot because you get to have the creative freedom to get whatever you're going through at the moment down. It's just a lot more creativity. When you're doing something advertisement-wise it has to be very commercial looking and you work with tons of clients. That's great because you'll still use your own input as to what you want for certain editorials and stuff, which is the creative side of it. With the fine art, it's your own thing. Coming up with your own vision, then being able to execute the vision and create a great image with that."
—Michelle Engberg: Professional Photographer

Can you identify your trifecta? One of the words on the list should be something that generally recharges you. At least one of those things should be a word to define the work you love to do (currently or in the future). Ideally you would include how you make money, and that would be something you enjoy. If you're not there yet- no problem. Make that the goal. Then look for a common thread or larger theme that ties two or more of these words together. Here are some examples of people who are doing what they love by incorporating multiple passions.

Mayra Ramales is pursuing a degree in Communicative Sciences and Disorders, with a minor in Media, Culture and Communication. She describes her WHY and the connection between her career and passions.

> *"Everything I do has to do with the ability to hear- your ears. Because if I couldn't hear, I wouldn't be able to write about all of this music. It all starts with your ears. I've worked with deaf children and I really fell in love with them. I want to find a way to mix both my love for music with my love for deaf culture and deaf people, the deaf community. In the future I want to find a way to help the deaf community experience music... to have everyone experience music and the arts, no matter what you're able to do."*
>
> *-Mayra Ramales: Founder &*
> *Manager of theSoundLive.com*

> *"I went and got my Master's in Psychology because I feel like when you're doubtful about things, you should always just go learn more. Whether it's an official degree or reading a bunch of books, you should always just learn more so you can figure out what answers can come to you. I've always been interested in psychology. I figured that could work for anything, no matter what I decide to do... When I was done with that, it just became clear to me that while a lot of my clients that I helped, I would write their bio but then I get an email at two in the morning that said, 'I'm on tour and I miss my boyfriend. What do I do here? Hey,*

I'm working with a band in the studio and I'm confused about what to do about copyrights. How should I attack that?' Asking me all these things. There's a lot of feelings, it was a big emotional roller coaster when you're a creative person. Let me take the psychology that I've learned and the exercises I've learned on how to stay grounded and focused– and mix that with the music business knowledge that I already have. Alas, The Rock/Star Advocate was born."
–Suzanne Paulinski, Mindset coach for
musicians & industry professionals

"I think it's very important to always test those labels. There is a value for you setting that label for yourself but then that label becomes a limitation. I had a very similar experience myself where I did stunts in Australia for a couple of years. Then I just kind of got bored of doing the same training, doing the same thing. It's a very small community over there. I was just basically spinning my wheels so I said that I'm kinda done with stunts, so I put it on the backburner.

Then I wrote my book, because I said I'm gonna try teaching for a bit. So, I started running workshops, wrote my book and worked with a lot of kids– disadvantaged youth. That was really colorful and creative for me because you can't predict kids. So, I'm still trying to be on my edge and not plan. I still want to have these new random experiences. But then my green card came through and I felt like the universe was saying 'come on Brett, time to get back into stunts again'. Here I am now in Hollywood because of this visa that I got. The opportunity was basically forced upon me, which I set up years ago and finally it's come. I'm doing these things that don't seem related, teaching and stunts.

Then I finally woke up to the relationship one day which is helping people overcome their fears. Now it makes total sense in hindsight... Teaching and stunts- they're so different yet so similar. I've come to realize now that everything really is the same. You can connect the dots with anything."
        -Brett Solomano: Hollywood Stuntman,
                Author, Speaker and Coach

If you are having trouble tying two or more of these words together in your trifecta, that is okay. The link is not always obvious. Try thinking about your WHYs and start performing actions that help you be the person you want to be. How can your work make a greater impact than just your wallet?

Alex Bondarev is a volunteer musician with the non-profit "Musicians on Call" which brings music to hospitals.

"I think we as artists have this fairy tale or this grandeur fantasy of playing an arena and how good that must feel. I think when artists spend some time with a child who hasn't been around anyone for a few days because they've been really sick- it's just them and their mom hanging around in a hospital room and you're there playing a couple of songs for them. You see their eyes light up, and you see the mom pulling out the phone to record you. It's an incredible feeling. This is just one of the nicest things you can do. I can't say enough good things about 'Musicians on call'." It's just really humbling and I think it's one of those things... You have these songs you want to share with people, and here you have these people who would just love to hear your song more than anything else. This is what they need right now. They feel like they're getting a private concert. It's one of the most humbling and rewarding things I've ever done...

Think of what other things you can do with your music that can help along the way, and make it a win-win situation. So obviously when you're a struggling artist, I get it, it's really hard to be heard, to be noticed. That's the most primal thing of all artists is to ask people to listen to my songs. I made this awesome thing. If you just combine that, and step away from the act of making this awesome thing for a second and change that into 'I made this awesome thing and how can I do some good with it?' If you combine those two things I think you'll go a lot further."
-Alex Bondarev: Refugee & Indie Singer-Songwriter from The Bronx

Your trifecta will emerge once you are on the right path, and it might change over time. I do not believe anyone is just one thing, that's why three is a magic number. Two is also okay, but I challenge you to think of a third unrelated passion, and how you can use it to your advantage. We are all multi-faceted and it is this variety in our life that makes us unique human beings. If we can tie together multiple passions, that is when we feel the most ease. That is why the life trifecta all stems from LOVE. We should connect to our work with our heart.

"When I went into crowdfunding, I did it for the wrong reason. I did it obviously to prove it wrong, that's definitely the wrong reason, but I also did it for the money. I was like, 'I could use $5,000.' Obviously, that's what crowdfunding is. You ask people for money. Then I realized when I started getting a lot of these contributions from strangers that I had just been talking to for a few months on Twitter, and most of my money came from Twitter, not even from family and friends... When I realized that, I literally had to shut down for a day and process this. That's

when I figured out, I'm going about this harder rather than smarter. I'm doing it for money when I shouldn't be doing it because of this community. As soon as I started working and giving to the community, then just like going with the flow, you give, you get. That's when it clicked. I was like, 'this reminds me of Daoism a lot'. I went back to my Tao Te Ching, which is the Daoist book. I started reading that. It was helping me to really see this crowdfunding thing was not about funding, but about the word that comes right before the funding, which is the crowd. If you make it about that, the funding is a byproduct that comes."
-John T. Trigonis: Filmmaker, Poet & Indiegogo's Head Film and Creative Campaign Strategist

One of my favorite speakers is Tara Brach. Her meditations and podcasts are really inspirational. I connected specifically with her ideas about intentions. Essentially, she says that our intentions can change how we feel. As a teacher, I can go into each class with the intention of making money, and just look for the highest paying jobs. Or, I can teach with the intention of helping others, inspiring young people and giving them a way to express their creativity. Having these positive intentions open me up for more valuable opportunities. I am excited to teach because I am fulfilling my good intentions. When I see a student truly learning and growing, it makes me feel great. Meanwhile when I get a paycheck, that's nice, but there is always another. Money is not my source of pride or self-worth. It just doesn't feel the same way as when we are doing something for the money. If we focus on our intentions rather than our actions or our income, we can always succeed because intentions are our way of BEING. Actions are things we do or perform. Income or fame is a social construct.

Both teaching and video production require a large amount of flexibility, essentially going with the flow, or making the best of your situation. At first, I used to be disappointed when I didn't stick to my lesson plan, but then I started focusing on my intentions to teach my students about values of teamwork, flexibility and storytelling. Now I am much more excited to teach each class, and it is a more enjoyable process. Give yourself an opportunity to succeed every day by focusing on your intentions rather than the actions you cannot control.

> *"I don't have a goal when I write, other than to be honest. Sometimes that means a song is not gonna be so happy. I'll write songs that are really deep, dark and heavy. I think it helps me deal with those emotions that so many of us suppress. My only goal is to be honest and generally that comes out positive and happy. I lean more towards, what's the meaning you can take away from this hardship? What's the light at the end of the tunnel? If an artist isn't making you feel good at the end of the day, or if a work of art isn't making you feel somehow better about your life- then you're just wallowing in self-pity… I'll know I have a good song on my hands or a good lyric when I'm scared to sing it. It's been a compass for me- feeling like this is really personal and wondering, 'should I say that?' If that's the question, then I think 'yes, I should' because a lot of people usually relate to that more than any of the other general stuff."*
> *-Alex Bondarev: Refugee & Indie Singer-*
> *Songwriter from The Bronx*

Speaking of flexibility, remember that it is okay to change your trifecta as you grow. This is not a lifelong formula for everyone. If you can't identify three things, that's okay. I am simply encouraging you to have a hobby that revitalizes your energy, and some variety in the tasks you perform for money. Having multiple skill-sets means multiple streams of income, and if one industry changes drastically or is not right for you anymore, there is always that other skill-set you can rely on.

> *"I'll be out of the army in probably a year because I've done that and my variety-seeker ways are telling me let's go see what the world has to offer. I don't know what that is but I love the fact that I don't know and I love the fact that my life will change and I will try something new. The possibility, the unknown and there's no obligations and limitations is a good feeling. Some variety seekers let that cause them anxiety but it is absolutely the way you think about it, and how you let your mind convince you to look at that situation as this ominous deep pit you're gonna fall down, or this limitless possibility of different things that you can be doing. It's all about mindset."*
> *-Alex Wood, co-founder of HoneLife*
> *and the Variety Seeker Tribe*

If you feel stuck or unsure of your next move, try using different muscles. That's where the third piece of your trifecta is really helpful. Find something you enjoy doing that is completely different. For me, drawing and painting is a non-technical thing that takes me away from the computer, and is non-verbal. I'm not putting together puzzle pieces of an edit, or speaking to a group, or organizing my thoughts to write a script. I simply get my hands dirty and start moving around colors on a canvas. It is a different skill and mindset that I am using. Janis Vogel and I discuss this theory on the LoudaVision podcast. Specifically, we were talking about the book "In the Blink of an Eye," by Walter Murch which is about the art of video editing.

> *"It's actually a really good and almost spiritual book. He says, 'bees find their way back to the hive more easily when they go*

further away from the hive.' If you try to get bees back into the hive by putting it two feet away from the hive, they won't find their way back. You have to really do something different sometimes to unlock the emotional potential of the scene."
-Janis Vogel: Professional TV & Film Editor

"That's like taking that walk outside when you're feeling burnt out with the project, you're using different muscles and senses and all this stuff. Seeing something in nature could spark an idea for the bio you were writing... using your body in a different way and stepping back, 100% it's a really healthy thing to do."
-Suzanne Paulinski: Mindset Coach for Musicians & Industry Professionals

Sometimes we just need to reframe our form of thinking all together, by giving ourselves a challenge. Turn the negativity of whatever we are going through, into a way to help others, and exercise a new skill set.

"I started pitching different television and film projects in 2013, and I would get so far and then for some reason it wouldn't go on air. So, I would feel rejected and it stopped me from the pitching project for at least four or five months on that project- and then I would pick up another project, develop a completely different show and set out on the journey again. I had realized that I can't continue to do this, to not pitch for four or five months is not gonna work well for my career. I set out on a journey to pitch 100 times because I wanted to rise above rejection. I wanted to get used to hearing rejection, going back out, fixing the issue, going back out again as fast as I could. It was through that

process that I learned 'NO' is not universal. So, what's not good for one network or studio house, producer/writer/ whoever that I'm pitching- it's not the same with everyone else. It doesn't mean that my project doesn't work. It means that it's just not right for where I had it, or they can't take any more projects. I've learned to not take it so personally."
-Squeaky Moore, Author of "100 Pitches, Mistakes I've made so you don't have to"

"One of the first things I tell people to do is continuous movement. What variety seekers tend to do is sit and wallow. They just sit there and think, but don't create any action or movement. You have to continue movement whatever that is. It could be physical movement, getting out of the house, or it could be movement online and finding a cause. What are your skill sets? What are your talents? Find a way to use them. It doesn't have to be something you're gonna do forever but get online and start making a movement. What's in your local community? What's a cause that's going on? Do you volunteer at all? Just bounce around and create opportunities. What that does is it builds more choices for you. Opening up potential avenues for careers and trying everything."
-Alex Wood, co-founder of HoneLife and the Variety Seeker Tribe

"We've got this comfort zone. It can be drawn as a circle on a map, or a circle on a piece of paper. You're in the middle and you have this circle above or around you. People don't even often approach the edge of the bubble and they just go about their 9-to-5. They have their hobby. They have their partner. They do those three things, and if they're

really on the edge they might have a little side business too. The bubble is there but if you don't hit the edges of your bubble all the time, your comfort zone is gonna contract on you. I see people who aren't even very old but their comfort zone is very small. I try to approach the edge of my comfort zone every day. I'm the kid that never grew up and still loves to take a dare. I think it's very important to keep that as an adult, obviously be more mindful and aware about it. People need to be pushing the edge of their comfort zone every day. Be confident and push your limits."

-Brett Solomano: Hollywood Stuntman, Author, Speaker and Coach

CHAPTER 14

WHAT'S HOLDING YOU BACK?

Figuring out your ideal career path is all about self-reflection and a positive perspective. If you can master your own mind, you can become self-aware, and make the most informed decisions. You have to believe that you can achieve the goals you set for yourself. Sometimes fear, negativity, ego, perfectionism or lack of focus can hold us back. Let's dig deep into these, starting with the single biggest cause of self-sabotage: FEAR.

> *"Fear shows in your thoughts when you have self-doubt or you talk yourself into or out of things based on a fear. Particularly I think fear is a lack of familiarity. Fear ties into procrastination quite a bit. They're not the same, they are kind of similar in many ways but different. Procrastination can be a lack of clarity and fear can be that as well where you're seeing something new and perceiving it before it happens. This happens particularly when you're overreaching for something. So, you're performing outside your capabilities."*
> *-Brett Solomano: Hollywood Stuntman,*
> *Author, Speaker and Coach*

"Practice is how you lose all your fears."
—Michelle Engberg, Professional Photographer

"I think that people are afraid of success. I see people that
are so talented but they just keep doing the same thing."
—Gabrielle Hawkins, Filmmaker

We are definitely afraid of success. I don't think that's true for everyone, but certainly for the people who do not have a clear definition of what success is to them. It's time to stop defining success by our bank account, job, physical abilities, or outer appearance. Ask yourself: What do I uniquely bring to this world? Those are my innate qualities that lead to personal success. Those qualities are the weapons that will slay the dragons within us. I know that if I put love and good intentions into an action or task, it will grow. I will succeed because I will be proud of my effort. If I define my own success, I will never fail.

We see other people and compare what they have to what we have. Automatically they become the poster-child in our mind, for success. If we are lazy about our definition of success, and just accept it to be what everyone else tell us it is, then we will never achieve it. This is ENVY. This often manifests as comparing myself to other people. What have they achieved that I have not? What do they have that I don't have? We're comparing things that don't equal happiness- material things such as money, fame, clothes, cars, etc. Envy serves no purpose but to keep us down, feeling bad about ourselves. My envy stems from self-doubt. It came up a lot for me when I was first dealing with some physical injuries that made it hard to do my job the way I used to. In this case I was comparing my present self to my past self, worried about how I'm going to make more money than I made in the past. No wonder I was disappointed. I was in competition with a younger, healthier version of me. Comparison and competition are the killers of hope.

"I think what happens is a lot of the times we do the whole comparison thing. That starts to eat at us. At least for me, that's when I tell myself, 'I'm not accomplished and I'm not any of this stuff.' When I teach it to my clients that are going through that, I say to them first off, 'Define what success means to you because it's going to be different for everybody'. Some artists might define success as for example, if they're musicians, it might be selling a certain amount of records or playing a certain venue or getting to collaborate with a certain tier of musician. What does that mean to you? Once they figured that out, I ask them 'why' because a lot of the times they might say, 'success means I get signed by a label'. I say, 'But why?' They've never really reflected on it because that's just what they're told, that's just what they know about the industry... I know plenty of artists that are making it their full time job and they're not signed to anything. There are other ways to do it but people, again, don't know what they don't know until they know it."
                                        -Suzanne Paulinski, Mindset coach for
                                        musicians & industry professionals

"It's like we are in this race, this competition. Even for me starting my private practice, I had to remain focused on what I believe, what I want in order to be successful. I had to not be distracted by competition. There's so much pressure in life- blogging, content, Facebook, social media and that's a lot to handle. The way I remain focused is by asking myself why I'm doing what I'm doing. What is my main purpose today? Sometimes you can't go through your whole to-do list and that's okay. We put so much

pressure [on ourselves] and that pressure takes a toll."
-Arta Cakaj, MS, LCAT: Wholehearted Art Therapy

"[Trying modeling] is a terrifying experience. I had a lot of friends tell me that I should be a model and try this. I'm 5 feet 1 , so I can't do certain modeling like fashion runway or advertising modeling because they need girls with longer legs. I kind of also wanted to show women that you don't have to be a certain requirement in order to be beautiful. So, I wanted to really push that. Beauty can come in any size and wherever you are in your life, as long as you start thinking about yourself in a more positive way. I also wanted to learn how to pose models better. It really helps because you get to learn what you're doing on the other side of the camera and how I can generate emotion through there. I've already been in three publications for my fine art pieces, with my modeling. Now I know on the other side how hard it is to get that pose right, that expression, that feeling... It's becoming easier for me to get the model in that frame of mind."
-Michelle Engberg: Professional Photographer

We often have assumptions about ourselves, and can be very harsh in assigning a definition to who we are. For example, just like Michelle, I used to think I was solely a behind-the-scenes person. This changed when my friend Lenina encouraged me to be on camera for a few videos as part of our 'Women of Action' YouTube series. It was really hard for me and I felt very uncomfortable. For at least five years, I had told myself constantly that my personality was not outgoing enough to be a host. This experience, and Lenina's encouragement to host the 'WoA podcast' with her, helped me question my own assumptions of myself. So, it is not always others that will put us in a box and categorize us, or write us off for an opportunity. Sometimes it is our own assumptions, and the fact that we don't question them. By challenging that assumption, I had about myself, I was able to gain the confidence I needed to start the LoudaVision Podcast- which inspired this book. Challenge the definition you have of yourself, and you will go places you never imagined. We often hear the saying "fake it till you make it." In this case, we are not faking anything, just pushing past fear. We are giving ourselves a chance to succeed. That success gives us confidence exponentially because we know we can be anything we put our mind to, and more.

> *"Keep on looking for different things. Keep on getting different photography jobs even if it's not exactly what you want. If you're a fashion photographer and have to do weddings. Every single different job that I've had, I've done schools, kids, weddings... they all taught me different aspects of photography. I use them still to this day so it's really beneficial for you beyond just a paycheck. Take photos and find companies that are willing to hire you to start out, or might teach you. There are a lot that will do that and you can still get paid for it. Find different ways to make money. Go online and do research, network with people... If you have the drive, and don't give up, you're eventually going to make it. The drive is gonna give you possibilities to meet new people and take you to places you never even imagined. In anything you do, you're gonna see results if you work hard."*
> *-Michelle Engberg: Professional Photographer*

Don't be fooled into thinking you are too good for something. I have heard a lot of filmmakers comparing wedding videography for example, to feature films. They don't see the skill or the art that goes into making wedding videos. They don't see how hard it is to break into that industry and how competitive it is. This assumption is deadly for the naysayer's wallet- because wedding videography generally pays more than being a production assistant on a feature film. Also, you get to be a part of someone's special day, and create something with heart. Not every feature film has such a positive outcome. I felt a similar way about news and documentary production for a long while, because it is not as prestigious in the eyes of the feature film connections I had from college. After being exposed to both industries, I have realized which one is right for my personality and my lifestyle choices. It is not about prestige or name-dropping. If you can master a skill and become successful in an industry, you have less time to compare yourself to others. Remember that success even in this example is not just about money. It is about living up to our own ideals and being who we want to be. If we live by other people's standards, we fail. Don't listen to other people judging your career choices, if it is right for you. We can never live up to another person's dreams.

From coaches with general advice, to friends, to that nosy relative who insists on telling you what you should be doing with your life… Stop clinging to other people for permission to try something new. It's okay to fail or give up at something that isn't working. It's okay to change your mind. You don't have to explain yourself to anyone. We've all heard before that "happiness is a journey not a destination," yet we still insist on plotting out every moment of our lives. Then we beat ourselves up when things don't go according to plan.

> *"Set goals and deadlines to stick to. Follow through on an idea, all the way, even when you get stuck. Never be afraid to drop an idea, to pivot or put something on hold if you get really stuck. But I had to learn to always name the reason why I was stuck and by clarifying the problem I was able to then come back to it when the solution presented itself."*
> *—Brett Solomano: Hollywood Stuntman,*
> *Author, Speaker and Coach*

"See yourself more like a fluid. You're gonna change. What we want right now might not be what we want in a few years from now, and that's okay. Give yourself permission to fail, even if things don't work well but the fact that you're trying and going after something you really want so bad will release all that pressure. You will find a way to make it work. And if you fail, that's okay. I went through this myself. Going into private practice was really between having a full time job or having a full time private practice. I always wanted to have my private practice. The reason is because it gives me so much freedom to do what I want. I can mold and tailor things that I want. It gives me that freedom of not being constrained to one approach or one style or all the bureaucracy that's out there. So, with this I can get rid of all that and just focus on the individual I'm working with. Find your priority: why do you want to do what you want to do? If money is not an issue, what else is holding you back?"
—Arta Cakaj, MS, LCAT: Wholehearted Art Therapy

A few years back, I decided that I wanted to work in TV sitcom production. So I went on a journey of curiosity to create my own pilot, which in my mind, would help me break into this industry. I considered enrolling in a graduate degree that would help me create this show, but I am glad I didn't. I just didn't want to commit to years of writing spec scripts, when I already knew this is not the task I want to do each day. I entered a large number of competitions for fellowships and programs that would teach me how to get into the TV industry.

The intention behind my wanting to create a TV series was so I had a legitimate excuse to leave my university job. I wasn't thinking about having to move across the country, or have a lifestyle that wasn't right for me. My intentions were wrong. After spending two years learning about TV series production, screenwriting, and pitching, I can say that it was worth the experience. I have all this additional training that I can use to help my teaching and video production career. I also have made great connections and met wonderful people that I truly enjoyed working with. Most importantly, thousands of dollars spent on creating my pilot has taught me that I do NOT want to be a TV series creator. It might have felt right for me two years ago, even one year ago, but it isn't right anymore. The key here is molding our ideas to fit our new goals, and using what we learned to get us there.

> *"Tyler Perry that idea. Tyler Perry will take a stage play, make it a movie, and that same show goes to TV for seven seasons. Same play, same themes, same characters then goes from a film to TV. You have to create addendums for it so that if it doesn't go one place, I can make it a web series, I can do my own thing with it... Can it live on a digital platform? You should always be flexible, but go for you goal. Open your mind up to other possibilities and then that's where the flexibility comes into play."*
> *-Squeaky Moore, Author of "100 Pitches, Mistakes I've made so you don't have to"*

> *"If you're a filmmaker, you're going to take that project down and you're going to reach in your back pocket and pull out the next idea. A filmmaker always has a next idea. Unless there's this person who just wants to make a film. That's the person that's probably not going to make movies for a living. You've got to have more ideas than one."*
> *-John T. Trigonis: Filmmaker, Poet & Indiegogo's Head Film and Creative Campaign Strategist*

"I wrote a play called Brownsville Bred that was very well received. It was sold out all the time in every venue that it ever played at, and yet still I never felt like I got everyone I wanted to see it, to see it. So, I knew I had to produce something where I could just send a link to people and say 'this is my voice, this is who I am'. So, I decided that the best way and most affordable way to do that is with a web series."
                                        –Elaine Del Valle: Film & TV
                                           Director, Producer & Actress

"It's a little scary because when you put something out there, you're kind of bearing your soul in fine art. You're putting your stuff out there for other people to critique. It's a little hard but my motto is that I don't like describing too much of the personal stuff that I was going through with the piece. I let other people relate so they can make up their own stories from it. Everybody interprets things the way their life is so I wanted to share that with everybody, and make them feel like they're not alone."
                                        –Michelle Engberg: Professional Photographer

Michelle's point about fine art definitely relates to my experience in pitching my TV series. Since my series idea was self-reflective and based on my own experience in my career, it became really hard to separate myself from it. At this time, I am not someone who has multiple ideas for different shows. I can surely "Tyler Perry" my few ideas into different formats, but what I love is production. Everything else feels forced and unnatural for me, and does not lead to my ultimate goal. If I had kept on this path, I could have learned to become good at pitching and writing screenplays, but I didn't want to. Sometimes the best thing for us is to see an experience for the value we got out of it, and to move on in a different direction. The key is flexibility in our mindset, and we can surely apply this to our career choices.

> "Architecture was a passion of mine until I learned more about the logistics behind the profession. It wasn't until about my third year [in college] where I realized that this may not actually be the thing for me. Mostly from a point of view of that I wouldn't be content doing that for the rest of my life, then there's also the financial component whereas I wouldn't actually be able to take care of myself and my family- because that's always been a goal of mine. I need to do something whereas I'd be able to give back and take my family out of the hood, for lack of a better word. That goal for me is first and foremost. The reason I continued on and got a degree in architecture was because my grandmother really, really pushed me and really wanted me to become an architect. It wasn't until mid-way through college where I had the courage to tell her that I'm only doing this for you. My passion 100% and I feel like my calling, is music. But I will continue and get this degree because I know how important it is to actually have a degree, to have some sort of proof of an education."
> -Teraj: Actor, Model and Musician

What else is holding us back? For a lot of people, it is money. There is a whole chapter in this book about money so if you think that is an excuse, go back and re-read. Aside from money, we have assumptions about life in general. We assume we have to work 40 hours per week. We assume we have to live in one place our whole lives. We assume that we will be happy if we have a big house, then find out we are just as unhappy when we get that house. We assume that other people's lives are perfect until we look closer. Question these assumptions by thinking about where they came from. Then challenge these same assumptions.

> "Things aren't always what they seem to be. I challenge my clients to challenge these preconceived ideas that we are fed. Like beliefs that if I lived in Italy, a renaissance painter would be birthed out of me. That might be your own truth so you should follow your bliss. But sometimes it's human nature to seek a sense of pleasure and chase after what appears to be the source of happiness, when really what is a source of pleasure cannot be found in those external circumstances or conditions. They might come from a state of mind. I'm challenging myself to see what a vacation gives me, and can I provide that to myself here, moment to moment? Do whatever it is to activate my mind, to inspire my mind so I'm not depending on traveling, not dependent on a partner, I'm not dependent on a certain job. But rather I can go there in my own mind- at will."
> -Anahita Moghaddam: Mindfulness Coach & Speaker, Neural Beings

> "Values we are taught from a very young age, with family. 'Do this. Don't do that.' We're taught to always cross the road at the crossing but we're not really taught why. It's through those kinds of actions we're taught that we have to follow authority, or that we always have to stand by our family's sides. We start getting fear when we don't follow the directions of our family. That's not the same for everyone, that's just a small portion of society. So, I definitely think that fear is very different for everyone based on the values that you have growing up, the actions you take as a child and the positive or negative experiences you have. Fear can definitely be overcome. Fear is very similar for a lot of

people and it's about mindfulness, about awareness, and it's about being able to capture your thoughts and rationalize them. Talk to yourself. When it talks back again, you have a language and a solution for the problem that your mind can often present... You need to be able to systemize and watch your mindset and the voices that kick up, and the fears. The strategies that I offer for that in my coaching and training is the ability to question yourself. When a thought comes up, ask if it's rational or not. Start questioning it. Ask 'do I know this to be true?' or 'how did I overcome this last time?', 'how has someone else overcome this?' You can start questioning it. Especially when it comes to reality. Is this really true? Is this really going to happen?"

-Brett Solomano: Hollywood Stuntman,
Author, Speaker and Coach

"You are not confined to your past or your current circumstances. You can actually get up and get out of your current situation, no matter where you come from. I grew up with super humble beginnings in Miami, we grew up very poor. There were a lot of naysayers especially growing up that would always tell me that I won't be able to do this, that I wouldn't amount to anything... 'You're from the hood and that's all you're ever gonna know.' I was just always against that. I always told myself that I would get out and just work my butt off. And I found that it was through education– that was the vehicle to get out. Just continuing to never give up on your goals."

-Teraj: Actor, Model and Musician

You are not the only person who holds yourself back from achieving your goals. Perhaps the world's most famous artist,

Leonardo DaVinci often struggled to finish his paintings. His biography says that he had trouble seeing a project through to its completion. This was because he preferred to conceive a project more so than executing it. He was so much a perfectionist that his ideas far exceeded his capabilities in real life. It is not arrogant to compare our own creative process to those of famous artists. I mention DaVinci, and I will also mention Michelangelo, who I also read about, to give you a look into the common mental blocks that stop even the most talented and recognized artists from succeeding in every project. We have to look at the big picture in order to understand how our own mind works.

If we are going to quit something, that's okay. Let's think about why we are giving up? Is it because we are too much of a perfectionist, like DaVinci? Or is it because we are afraid of our own success? Are we afraid of criticism (from ourselves and others) that might come with sharing the work that we put so much of our heart and time into?

In a biography about Michelangelo, I found it interesting to hear how he used spite for the people who hired him, as motivation to complete projects. These rich patrons were paying him to create paintings and sculptures for their churches or villas. Just like we sometimes encounter in this modern day, working for others can sometimes be contentious. It can become a process that is despised, and filled with a lot of emotion, where our creative side fights the part of us that needs to make money. Michelangelo is known for having painted his patrons as horrifically ugly demons on the ceiling of the Sistine Chapel. I love this story because unlike DaVinci, who often left projects unfinished even when there was money on the line, Michelangelo used his anger to actually inspire him to finish. Michelangelo was said to not like most of the work he created for patrons. He was also overly critical of his own work, obsessing over the minor flaws where others saw beauty. Sound familiar?

As artists and creatives, we can be our own worst critic. But is that criticism being used to positively motivate us to finish? Or are we looking for any excuse to give up? Remember that perfection is not attainable, it is a scale. We can only hope to finish in a place that is closer to perfection than imperfection. Even if we don't succeed in a traditional sense, and two years of our work, like my TV series, does not produce any tangible rewards- we have to be proud of ourselves for finishing. We can still take lessons and benefits from the experience, even if it is not perfect or didn't bring us to the place we expected to end up.

"You launch a campaign, you run it. Whether it's successful or not, if you're putting in the work, you're spreading the word. You're trying to get it out to a lot of people and it just doesn't hit the goal, that's fine. If it does hit the goal, it's even better. What it does, if there's an investor looking and they see this and they like the idea, and they see that you've made some traction on it. I've seen people get money from investors because the investor found them on a site like Indiegogo... I would say that's a direct result of the awareness factor. A lot of times people get let down. It's like, 'Oh, I did all this work. I was promoting and promoting and promoting. I didn't hit my goal.' But you built up your Twitter following. You built up your Facebook fan page. You've done all this other stuff. That's a success too. That's the part that we don't fully see a lot of times... That's why I look at success as not did it hit its goal, but with whatever you raised, can you make this move forward? If the answer is yes, awesome. You're just as successful as if you hit that campaign goal."
-John T. Trigonis: Filmmaker, Poet & Indiegogo's
Head Film and Creative Campaign Strategist

"For me I had to let go of- I still struggle with it, I'm not gonna lie, but definitely putting it in its place- being a perfectionist. You can get caught up on the smallest of details. Just let that go."
-Teraj: Actor, Model and Musician

"We all have these goals that we want to achieve, and these things we aren't doing. As freelancers, creatives, artists and performers- there are always these other intangible goals we want. It's not laid out for us. Life is never laid out for creative types, for better or worse. We're always a glutton for punishment in that way but because of the lack of tangibility and lack of structure we often get stuck. We're procrastinating and planning and in a way protecting ourselves from our own success. We think that if we keep planning that everything will be fine. What I've found is that you definitely need to create momentum to keep working towards your goals. You've got to have little wins every day. Also that means you need to overcome little fears. Reach out to people, complete things- maybe it's 80% complete. You don't need to perfect it you just need to get it out there. That's a fear for many people, that protectionism that often creative types have."
-Brett Solomano: Hollywood Stuntman,
Author, Speaker and Coach

Perfectionism should not be idealized as an attribute of working hard. They are unrelated. Perfectionism is actually very negative because we are not having realistic expectations. It took me years as an editor to realize that no video is ever really complete. I was spending so many additional days and hours fine-tuning every second of a video in post-production. Meanwhile, most viewers aren't really paying as much attention as I am. At some point the details become lost. There is nothing wrong with giving yourself a deadline and doing your best in that timeframe. That is how I work now and I still create videos I am very proud of, without driving myself crazy.

> *"Editing is decision-making. Thousands of decisions a day. I would say I've become faster, maybe not better, but a faster decision-maker since editing for this long. You just have to make one and then you'll find out whether it's right or wrong... Editing is very meticulous and very, very detail oriented. Then it also has to be totally reckless and unexpected and creative."*
> *-Janis Vogel, Professional TV & Film Editor*

> *"It's about finding a balance. It's about getting more discipline. More recently I've realized that I have to use my time wisely because there are only so many hours in a day. You have to work and pay the bills so I think about where can I cut back. Certainly there's social media and reading things that don't really matter that much. I love a good show so I'm totally a binge watcher on Netflix, HBO and stuff. But I'm really cutting back from that. At the same time I think there's something to be said for allotting yourself a certain amount of hours to work on something [with a cutoff]. I think it's a healthy practice and it makes your brain a little sharper I think as far as getting done what you need to. Somehow if I know I have three hours to work on this song and these lyrics, somehow it moves along a little better than when you have 12 hours and procrastinating for the first three. It's finding a balance and setting in place certain things that help you achieve your goals."*
> *-Alex Bondarev: Refugee & Indie Singer-*
> *Songwriter from The Bronx*

Some of us think that negative people are holding us back. This might be true, but only because we believe them.

"Keep at it! Someone is always going to have something to say. So if you receive negative criticism or feedback, don't let that get you down because everybody can't please everybody. Just define what you're niche is, really delve and tap into that, do your best to thrive at it and never never give up."
—Teraj: Actor, Model and Musician

"For me as I'm getting older and wiser, I feel like letting go of all that pressure and just be myself. It's your life and you're making these decisions because this is what works for you. It's okay that maybe we're not pleasing our parents, our competitors. Just taking the pressure off and remaining focused on what is giving you joy right now. What is making you work on this project, because you're passionate about it? Just go with it and see where it takes you. Don't get distracted by the negative comments and negative people in your life. Just really nourish that which is giving you pleasure and happiness."
—Arta Cakaj, MS, LCAT: Wholehearted Art Therapy

"We're selective about the food that we eat, the shows we watch, the people we eventually end up with. Be as selective with your business partners. You're going to be around this person for many hours making important decisions. It could make or break your business, and potentially damage your brand."
—Lina Lansky, MBA: Filmmaker

Personally, I believe that a degree of skepticism and the ability to identify why you are unhappy is a good skill to have. That skepticism keeps our perspective on the bigger picture. However there is a line between healthy self evaluation and full blown negativity. Take the time to identify your negativity triggers, and rather than trudging through your day in this state, choose to shift your focus to accomplish tasks that do not require too much of you emotionally. This is the best time to complete those tedious tasks, where you do not have to interact with others. Or perhaps you might have the time to do something for yourself that will shift your mood. For me that is watching a movie, playing with my cat, or creating art. There are multiple ways to find your inner happy place. Some will suggest meditation, miracle mornings, mindfulness, etc. I choose gratitude as my practice because even if I am in the worst mood, if I think about what I am grateful for in my life, it lifts that cloud of crankiness. My mood shifts. Sometimes it is okay to be cranky and just take some time to decompress. We do not have to walk around 100% joyful and ecstatic all the time- that is not realistic.

"I can be negative too. We [all] have tendencies but I think it's a muscle you train. A good quote I heard recently is 'what's wrong is always available but so is what's right'. So it's just a matter of- sure there are a ton of really horrible things always happening, a ton of things we can't explain or make sense of. I think our capacity for good is just as great, if not much greater than our capacity for destruction or evil."
-Alex Bondarev: Refugee & Indie Singer-
Songwriter from The Bronx

"When that doubt comes in and that self-hatred of 'what am I even doing? Why would anybody work with me?' When you stop and think about it, it really creeps up... I started

to be more self-aware when those things would happen. It usually creeps up when I'm about to do something I've never done before or I'm about to do something really exciting that I have worked a long time for. It's when a big shift is happening. We start comparing and we start looking at what everybody else is doing and thinking, 'how can I even compare myself? I haven't done this, this or that. Here are all these other people doing amazing things'. When that comes up, the advice I always give for that is, remember that you're in your own lane. Nobody else can get in your lane. Imagine a highway with 1000 different lanes in it and you can't switch lanes. This is your path. You might look over to the other lane and see somebody else with a nicer car or whatever. They can't get to where you are. They might be looking over at you and finding things that you're doing that they wish they could do. When those things happen, start making a list of everything you've done, no matter how small it might be and just list everything. That's when the gratitude comes in, that's where the giver's gain attitude comes in. Get out of your own self-hatred and look around you and see who you can help, see how you can pay it forward because that gets us reenergize and that makes us feel like we attributed to somebody else's success. It reminds us of what we have to give."
—Suzanne Paulinski: Mindset Coach for Musicians & Industry Professionals

The goal is to be in a place where we feel emotionally balanced and unaffected by the outside world. Of course there are exceptions to this, and things will happen in our life that will make us very sad. It is okay to be sad at times. In these moments of sadness we should proactively look for the things in life that are linked to this emotion. If it is something that is under our control to change, like a bad job, or spending time with a negative person, then we should change it immediately. If it is a chronic problem, consider seeking professional help. For most, negativity is a choice and we can change it by adjusting our mental diet. This includes what we read either books, or even on our social media feeds. Our mental diet also includes the emails we are subscribed to, the videos we watch, podcasts we listen to, etc. Changing our mental diet takes time, however it can be done if we look critically at the media we consume, and actively work to change it. The facebook algorithm for example, keeps us in a bubble where we are seeing ideas similar to what we already believe, based on posts we like, share and comment on. Confuse the algorithm by actively searching for ideas that challenge what you believe, and subscribing to positive sources that will help you succeed.

Here is a short list of some of the most influential books I have read (in no particular order). These inspirational books helped me overcome my own negative tendencies and figure out what I really want in life.

- 'Breakdown Breakthrough' by Kathy Caprino
- 'Ego is the Enemy' by Ryan Holiday
- 'Jonathan Livingston Seagull' by Richard Bach
- 'No is a Four Letter Word' by Chris Jericho
- 'The Alchemist' by Paul Coelho
- 'The Confidence Gap' by Russ Harris
- 'The Gifts of Imperfection' by Brene Brown
- 'The Power of I Am' by Joel Osteen
- 'The War of Art: Winning the Inner Creative Battle' by Steven Pressfield
- 'Why We Work' by Barry Schwartz

On the LoudaVision Podcast, Gabrielle and I discuss our interpretation of the book "The War of Art" listed above.

"We're always going to have excuses as to why we're not doing something. I know I have a lot of them. I'm not feeling well or money issues, but you know what? I'm frickin' alive. Let me figure this sh** out. Let me finish this movie. The great thing about that book is that we can apply it to our art but also to life."
–Gabrielle Aliké Hawkins: Filmmaker

You will notice that I have not listed books about making money, getting rich or influencing others. I did read those books, but didn't find them to fit with my intentions. The goals they were aspiring to were not right for my personality. I encourage you to think critically when reading or consuming anything, even this book. If something doesn't work for you, it is okay to disagree. Question everything, test it out for yourself and modify.

Aside from books, you might also benefit from podcasts, videos and magazines that are inspiring. The media you consume should help you achieve your career goals, and mental goals too. Staying positive is a daily practice. This proactive approach helps me keep negativity from slipping into my mental diet.

I also would recommend Tara Brach's podcast and meditations available for free on her website. Additionally, Leo Babauta's 'Zen Habits' emails me wonderful messages that challenge my negative tendencies.

Most importantly, I just want to share that anyone can choose to be negative, even me. Everyone has good and bad moments. It is your choice how you bounce back from that negativity. I heard great advice from a bright young man I interviewed named Shawn, who had so much positive energy and a wonderfully inspiring personality. As a teen, he had an accident which paralyzed his legs. I asked him how he stays so positive despite being in a wheelchair. Granted, my question was self-interested at the time, as I was wallowing in negativity about some of my own physical limitations. Shawn said that he lets himself wallow and be negative for a maximum of five minutes each day. He lets it all out. After that, he has to be positive and go on with his life because he cannot change what he cannot control.

That day was very important in my life, having felt so negative for a long time over my back problems. I felt that I was a useless human being because my back injury wouldn't allow me to do camera-work at the time. What a ridiculous idea, in retrospect. I see now that feeling was completely driven by ego and my attachment to my identity as a camera-person. If we can change the definition of identity to the qualities we have and what we want to BE, rather than what we DO physically, we can have more confidence and hope for the future.

> *"You have to dig a little deeper into why you're fearful of moving forward. What I like to do, and there's an exercise in my book [Rock Star Life Planner] called The Doubt Dump. The Doubt Dump is really putting all those WHYs out there. I don't feel good enough because of this. Then flipping that. I call it flipping the script. If you feel, 'I'm going to create this film but I'm afraid that nobody's going to appreciate it.' Flip that. 'I'm going to make this film. At least one person is going to be touched by it and their lives could be changed by it. People are going to watch it and they're going to get such enjoyment out of it and escape their life for the next 90 minutes.' However you want to flip it, because the future is 50/50. The future can suck or the future can be amazing. The reality is it's probably going to be somewhere in between. Why do we always focus on it being horrible? We're just programmed."*
> *—Suzanne Paulinski, Mindset coach for musicians & industry professionals*

Find the people that inspire you, no matter who they are. Surround yourself by these people and the messages that help you be your best self. Most importantly, treat yourself well and practice positivity in your own mind. After all, our own voice is the one we hear most frequently. Let your own inner voice be positive and encouraging. Let it lift you up rather than hold you back.

"I think it's really important to know one's own needs. To be able to listen to one's own needs. If you're signing up to be an artist, there has to be some kind of mental hygiene that has to occur. Giving yourself self care, whatever you need to be your best.Inquiring within is one of my recommendations. It's about learning to speak the language of the body.

The way to learn is to first quiet down the chattering mind. To be able to distinguish between: When am I in my head? When am I dissociated from my body? When am I living solely on the concept of idea, personal narrative, constantly fabricating narratives, living on that realm? (which is complete hypothetical, complete illusory, disconnected from reality). Versus when am I in my body: What are the sensations that I am feeling in this moment? What are the emotions I am experiencing in response to the data I am perceiving, in response to ideas that are running through my head in my thoughts?

Having that sort of real time awareness of the body, being in that experiential state, and relating to one's environment through the body makes the experience of life so much richer, and makes us so much more conscious, and we are able to make decisions that are much more informed, that are more in line with what we really desire. Rather than to

take action from a place of habituation which is unconscious. Drawing on previous knowledge of what's comfortable and acting from that place, and recreating over and over the same limited experience of ourselves of space and time."
–Anahita Moghaddam: Coach, Speaker
& Founder, Neural Beings

CHAPTER 15

CREATIVITY + EXECUTION

You might not need to quit your current job in order to have the ideal career. It is possible to make the best out of the situation you are in, and use whatever we have at our disposal to help us grow. How horrible are the negatives on your career assessment list compared to the positives for this job? Could you maybe add something new as a part time job or volunteer opportunity on the weekends that would get you to where you want to be? Is it possible to adjust your schedule so you can have more work/life balance or give you time to pursue your other goals? Remember that introspection will guide you. Find out what's holding you back and change it. If you require a big change like quitting your 9-to-5 to become a freelancer, surely you will have enough information already from this book in order to make that decision. This chapter is about how to always be a creative genius, no matter how you make money. Since the LoudaVision Podcast is for creative people, I have gathered lots of advice from successful artists in many fields. You can use this information to guide your career choices, or as a way to help you find the creative outlet you hold just for yourself.

We dream up these creative ideas seemingly all day and night. We wake up with them, we write them down in the strangest places, and find inspiration from seemingly everywhere. What do you love to create? How can you bring it to life?

> *"It's a rewarding thing, especially when you don't know where it comes from. This is the creative process. This is art and art is life."*
> *-John T. Trigonis: Filmmaker, Poet & Indiegogo's Head Film and Creative Campaign Strategist*

> *"When you have an idea for something it will take you somewhere because it's where you want to go. Whether it's make a film, podcast, a project. When you open those doors, so many more things happen in your life… People are doing it because they cannot help it. We had to do it because the feeling wouldn't go away. The passion is stronger than your fear."*
> *-Magdalena Reilly: Documentary Filmmaker, Podcast Host, Minimalist & World Traveler*

> *"There are a few things that I do to stay creative. Always look for inspiration and beauty around you. Observation is also critical to the creative journey. Noticing things that inspire you will spark creativity as you troubleshoot issues or face design. Ask 'what if? or what could be?' Always pushing further into the problem and thinking outside the typical answer. What if a different approach will give you a better result. What could be instead of what is. Not only will this set you apart in the freelancing world, but it will also keep you energized as a creative. Always push the boundaries and keep learning. Lastly don't overthink, over design, or complicate things. Simplicity is difficult. It requires you to be intentional. So often we clutter the idea. Fight that urge and be simple."*
> *-Michael Woodward: Freelance Web Design/Development & Podcast Host*

If you have an idea for a creative project, find a way to execute it. Your voice is just as important as Hollywood filmmakers, or famous artists. Make sure you are clear on your intentions with the project, no matter what it is. There are so many rewards that come from executing your creative ideas: you might grow as a leader, an artist, meet new people or find your ideal career path. Alternatively, it might just serve as a great way to unwind. Almost everyone will get a sense of confidence and satisfaction by bringing an idea to life.

> "The key is everybody should get one chance at making their project. If they want to do everything, God bless them, they can do everything. But learn from that experience and take that to the next one and say, 'I really conquered this part of it and I was good at that and I enjoy doing that, but other parts I didn't really enjoy and maybe it could've been a lot better.' Hire the people that can help you accomplish things. Or if you don't want to hire people, trim it down to a point where you can do it by yourself properly."
> -Valentin Farkasch: Filmmaker & Photographer

Let's say you are a freelancer or entrepreneur and love your job, but some of the tasks you have to do each day are on the negative side of your career assessment list. The goal would be to outsource that task as soon as you financially can. If you can't afford someone, maybe hire an intern to help. Look at the negatives on your list and problem-solve how you can take them off your plate. If there are too many negatives and not enough solutions, that is a sign that you are not where you should be, or not thinking creatively. Remember that creating something is hard work. Just because it is art, doesn't mean it is easy. We can create projects that personally challenge us and help us grow in many aspects of our life.

The creative process can become more complicated if we are working as an artist. That would mean we are creating something for someone else, according to their wishes and parameters, in exchange for money. When someone else is funding a project or supervising it, we have much less control. It is harder to use the experience to help us grow and meet our own personal goals. However, we can still learn things from this process. In my experience, when creating videos for a client, I get to learn about a new subject. I also learn how to work with others, and be a better business-person.

When I created my short holiday film "Give a Little" for example, I was doing that for myself, and I had much more creative freedom. There was less explaining and asking for permission to try something new. The goals were set by me, and I had full responsibility for the outcome. I had to fund the project myself, and make all important decisions. It was a wonderful experience to be able to work with such a small crew, and play many roles. I was the camera-person, sound-person most of the time, director, and editor for this short holiday film. While I had help with writing, an assistant director, and immense help from the small cast and crew, it filled me with a lot of pride to be able to have my hand in so many aspects of this project. I asked for some feedback on graphics and special effects, but essentially, I was in charge of the final edit. I knew what I wanted to accomplish, trusted my skill, and I had the responsibility to make sure it succeeded. Each holiday season, I see the number of views for "Give a Little" go higher and higher on YouTube. This makes me feel great knowing that I can share this work with people all around the world. It is not restricted to only people who will buy it. This increases the impact it can have by making it available for more people to see. No strings attached.

> *"If I take that money equation out of it and just say I do whatever I feel like creatively. I just have ideas, I don't restrict myself in any of them. I just write them down and see what is practical at the moment. That gives me freedom to have better ideas. At least that's what I hope, and*

actually execute them because a lot of times there are ideas that are great, that you can do them, but they don't get done because you have to do other projects. The timing isn't right."
—Valentin Farkasch: Filmmaker & Photographer

When I was working full time I expected to have more availability to travel and create new independent projects as a freelancer. The reality is that freelancing is so unpredictable that there was no way I could schedule time for a video production of my own. I would either get called to film the next day, or next week. It was very hard to plan ahead. Also, the lack of steady income means that I could not afford to travel and invest in my own projects. My solution was to spend my freelance time writing this book, as it is a much more flexible and inexpensive process to write, than to create a video with a cast, crew and other expenses. Surprisingly, I had more ability to create my own projects when I was working full time, because of the stability. This lead me to really define the creative full time career that I dream of. I know that it is out there, and by having this experience on both sides of the fence, I have clarity to go towards that goal. My curiosity and love for learning is much stronger than the desire to work for myself.

For others, having a full time creative career might not be ideal. It is up to you to decide whether or not you want to be creative for money. This is an important question for many artists.

If you want to be creative, with no restrictions, take money out of it. You will truly be your own boss. However, do you have the money and time to invest in that creative project? Perhaps there is a grant or fellowship available to fund your idea. If not, challenge yourself to think of another way to exercise your creative juices that is not affected by your schedule and income. Use your creativity to be resourceful. Here are the benefits of creating a project for yourself.

"Luckily, I pay for it myself so I don't have to answer to anybody."
–Elaine Del Valle: Actress, Writer,
Producer & Casting Director

*"I wanted to be my own boss. It really was a quick idea
I had when I decided I want to start theSoundLive.
com. It was lingering in my mind for about a month
then I said I have to do it now. So, it was impulsive. I
came up with the name in five minutes. I had just met
a web designer... he just very quickly got me going. I
came up with the way I wanted it to look, the logo, the
name, just everything that I wanted to be featured on
this website. We just got to it and within a week I had it."*
–Mayra Ramales: Founder &
Manager of theSoundLive.com

Mayra started her own website by requesting permission to use the work she had previously done for other websites. Once they gave the okay, theSoundLive.com was up and running. Plus, Mayra had made connections that gave her access to concerts she could cover, and she built a network of content creators that would contribute to her site. So just because your creative work is being done for another outlet, or a client, that doesn't mean they wouldn't give you permission to use it for yourself.

Let the things you love to do, and what you do well or might want to learn, guide you to your next creative project. You can start out doing creative work for others but then turn it into your own thing. Modify the format, Tyler-Perry the idea, riff on it. I went through that same process when starting my podcast. I had learned podcasting techniques from my job at the time, and had co-hosted a podcast for 'Women of Action'. Then I realized that I wanted to have a show of my own on a subject of my choosing. At the time,

I was very nervous to try this, but I am so glad I took that leap. It was the perfect thing for me at a time when I was working for so many other people, and just frustrated at the collaborative process in general. With my own podcast, I am able to make all the decisions, and I am the person with the ideas. I finally felt that my effort was being used to create something for ME. It was a great way to exercise new skills and challenge myself while helping others with similar interests.

"As a creative person, you have to take risks. Most people feel that, 'oh, I'm not really a person who takes risk. That's for brave people, or that's for courageous people, or that's for artists or whatever.' The truth is, all of us are scared. Singing helps us break through a really deep fear of expressing ourselves. Once you break through that, it's like anything can happen. It releases you from that intense feeling of working on your art, working on your craft. You pour your heart and soul into these things and then you need release."
-Julia Amisano: Singing, Piano & Acting Teacher

"Everyone is creative in some form or another. Just try allowing yourself even thorough play to be creative. I think schools have changed the way children and teens see creativity and art because there's so much pressure in the end product, the grade, and then the teacher becomes an art critic. I think that takes the joy out of the creativity. I try to somehow repair that in my sessions, and just take the pressure off. It doesn't matter how it's going to look. As long as you are enjoying the process, the artmaking and you're getting messy. That's the beauty of it."
-Arta Cakaj, MS, LCAT: Wholehearted Art Therapy

Whatever your reason for creating your project, just do it. Don't let anyone stop you. More importantly, don't stop yourself.

> *"One of the hardest things about being an artist is motivating yourself through the day-in, day-out kind of stuff. It's not always easy. There are so many things that are easier than making good art. There are so many forces around us that will tell us that this isn't important, that this is secondary. Think about the toughest times in your life or when you're struggling through something. It's usually in those times that you go to a good movie, or a good song, or a good book. You confide in those things that artists created to get you through the hardest times of your life. They shape how you look at the world. So, imagine just if all those people [artists] chose not to do that because they thought something else was more important?"*
> *-Alex Bondarev: Refugee & Indie Singer-*
> *Songwriter from The Bronx*

We have to analyze how we connect to our creative work. Are we letting our work define us? Or are we using it to express ourselves?

> *"You can use art in a therapeutic way for yourself. I suggest to some of my clients that you can go home and use your journal to express your feelings. Or if you're anxious about something, doodle something about it. Just open your sketchbook and just doodle or write about it if you feel you don't want to express through a drawing, just write something about that build-up. There is a healing that happens just by making art. Sometimes you can understand your own art, and sometimes we just don't have that awareness. That's okay. Just the process of the artmaking is healing in itself. It's therapeutic. You can use art, writing and any*

form of creativity, even video, and make it therapeutic for you. Art takes you away from your reality into somewhere else. It can be in any form. It's just allowing yourself to be, and experience that. Just relax and enjoy the process."
-Arta Cakaj, MS, LCAT: Wholehearted Art Therapy

When I was first starting out in video production, I used to get my feelings hurt. Constructive criticism did not yet exist in my mind. Critique for one of my projects was always a personal attack on me as a person. Does this sound familiar? A lot of creatives struggle with this, and it sometimes stops us from sharing our work with others for fear of the negative judgement. At its worst, this fear can stop us before we even start our projects. It can prevent us from accomplishing anything.

In my first college film class, I had spent days tireless editing my film to perfection (in my mind). When I presented it to the class, the students were very kind to me. It was our professor who gave me a reality check. He nit-picked every cut that he didn't like, and mentioned everything he thought could be better. He was really on a roll. To me, I didn't hear his good intentions at the time. I simply said thank you with a stoic face, and the second I left class, I broke down. I proceeded to call a friend, who was an actor in this film, and told him how the teacher hated it, how it was garbage and I was going to fail. I questioned if I ever wanted to go back to class, let alone go back and re-edit the film. I was of course exaggerating, but this is how negative feelings can multiply. My friend gave me very good advice, and said that if just one person didn't like it, that didn't mean I should give up. He encouraged me to listen for the ways I can improve and fix the video, not just the judgement of it. I had felt mentally done with the project because I exhausted myself with perfectionism the night before. I was low on sleep and over-worked myself. This critique was exactly what I needed to toughen up and realize the reality of being an artist. Everyone is going to judge your work because it is art. Unlike so many other fields where the assignment is complete, with maybe a thank you, art always encourages people to give their opinion, even if we don't ask for it.

Depending on the nature of the project, we may have to share the work before it is complete, in order to meet a deadline or get input from our managers. In this case, an outside perspective can be helpful. Someone else might see a problem that we missed, or have a different viewpoint that gives one of our creative choices a new context. Having constructive input from a diverse group of critics can improve our work. However, we cannot take input on our work as a personal attack.

> *"It's so important on social media to share your process, let them in on why you're going to take a departure into another genre, whether it's film or music. Get on social media, explain to them. People that aren't creative don't get it. It's important that you explain to them, 'listen, I'm a creative person. I'm so glad you really liked my last project. I'm going to bring that same skillset with me to the next project but I want to try something a little bit different'. Ask them for their support. Ask them to come on this journey with you. Share the pieces of what this journey was about so that they can feel like it's not so scary, it's not so different."*
> *–Suzanne Paulinski: Mindset Coach for Musicians & Industry Professionals*

> *"Fear loves isolation. So, when you're in a group, celebrating successes and seeing each other's failures can really motivate you and keep you glued together."*
> *–Brett Solomano: Hollywood Stuntman, Author, Speaker and Coach*

On the other hand, having all this outside noise can severely confuse our message. Everyone has a different perspective on a project. If you are creating something for yourself, you don't need to ask for critique. Just complete it, present it and be proud of your work. Trust yourself to know when it is ready to share. But don't be surprised when other people have an opinion about your art. Their opinion doesn't define the value of your effort.

Since everyone will judge our creative projects, we have to keep our identity separate from the work we create. It is our work, but it does not define our value as a person. Connect to the creative process, not to the outcome of your work. Be proud of what you have accomplished, even if it is not perfect.

Filter out all the noise that tells you how you should complete your task. It is okay to research and look for advice, but just as I've said a million times, not everything works for every person. Do what is best for you. Everyone has their own creative process.

There are a lot of tutorials and advice articles out there on how to make a podcast. Most of them say you HAVE to do at least one episode per week, even two. When I started my podcast, I did not have the time for that. Even though I got a lot faster at creating my show over time, it just never felt right for me to do this type of weekly schedule. I wanted to make sure that the people I interviewed were relevant to the topic of creativity. I wanted guests that I was going to be excited to speak with, and people I can learn from. If I had approached it with the intention of making money, I would have just filled up my calendar with interviews. That would have produced more quantity but not much else. My intentions were to focus on the quality of my interview guests. This is how I made podcasting work for me. You can do the same in your creative endeavors. Do things at your own pace and in the way that helps you achieve your personal goals.

"The more I wrote, the more I started to find my own voice. It was very Latino-centric, and these are the stories that I want to tell. And if I was producing it on my dime, and I was directing it, and I was gonna be in it, this is the story that I want to tell. So, I had that gift to make those decisions to be the showrunner and writer as well. It just turned into something really special."
-Elaine Del Valle: Film & TV
Director, Producer & Actress

If you feel stuck, try taking a different approach. Riff on your ideas and let them evolve. There are no limitations to what your creative ideas can become if you let yourself explore. By thinking creatively, I am able to turn my interviews from the LoudaVision Podcast into this book. The content already exists, I am just looking for a new way to deliver it. You can do this with many of your ideas and projects. Re-packaging can help you break into a new industry, learn a new skill and challenge yourself.

Here is some of the best advice I have gathered regarding the creative process.

"What I've learned over time is that the most important thing is to be you. You don't necessarily have to know who YOU are. Just make the art that feels authentic and right to you. Eventually it'll find its own voice. Just do the art that you're always thinking about doing. Then build on the relationships that you have. Value those relationships, contribute to them.

Look for new relationships as far as new mentors, people you can learn from. Watch what other artists are doing and see how you implement certain thing that they're doing in a way that's your own. And service- see what area of life that your art speaks to or contributes to

that needs the help. Just be willing to contribute that."
-Alex Bondarev: Refugee & Indie Singer-
Songwriter from The Bronx

"So many people have so many great ideas. So, what really is going to set your idea apart. For me that's action. I create them."
-Elaine Del Valle: Actress, Writer,
Producer & Casting Director

"Never give up. Things don't happen overnight so through persistence just keep at it. If you're good at what you do, in due time, you're going to get recognition. It's just about staying in the game and just keeping at it."
-Teraj: Actor, Model and Musician

CHAPTER 16

WHAT MAKES YOU HAPPY?

Your chosen career should incorporate your WHY and challenge you to grow. That career should complement your lifestyle choices. You should also leave yourself time to enjoy life's rewards. When it comes to the big picture, only you know what choices you have to make, in order to live your most authentic life.

Freelance versus full time is just a detail of that larger lifestyle question. You surely have a lot of information to consider in your journey. Know that it is okay to change your mind over time. Freelancing might work for a certain number of months or years, and then you might want to go back to a 9-to-5. Our life changes and the choices we make should be indicative of what we learn about ourselves and what we need right now.

> *"When things change, every day you can put yourself into a great state. We all know that that state ends and all of a sudden, you have very dark thoughts and very self-defeating thoughts and your goals change. My goal is to get signed and now I got unsigned today. How am I still so confident? It's over time. It's the patting yourself on the back every day. You've got to learn to have patience with yourself.*

Thank God, I'm 25 and I feel like I'm still really early on getting that. When things change and when your goals change, that's okay. You know what I like to do? Listen to the wind blow. That's not in a nature-y weird way. Listen to the daily in-between moments. We're talking about in-between stand-up comedy moments on stage. It's all about timing to pop that giggle out of your audience. You've got to just listen to the sound of the wind, to the trees and the leaves blow. The events in your daily life, especially when you're in a time, a phase of upheaval, if you're in a pit of despair, if you're getting over something, if you're challenged, it's going to be even highlighted more. Your job is just to be aware and to be present and to imagine yourself over your head, six feet on the subway train car. You're not just in your own head, whether you're thinking really positively or negatively, you are listening to the different languages that are being spoken around you. You can be grateful for that, for being in a place where you're safe and where you have different languages. It's such a melting pot and safety, thank God.

If you're aware of the daily blessings, because they're really blessings too, you don't need the big yachts every day and the big Maserati's and the big functions to keep you happy, a thousand Instagram likes. You can just get a kick out of talking to an old guy for five minutes about his days as an actor or whatever it is, opening the door and getting that sense of satisfaction. That five-year plan, you just had that overarching sense of confidence. When things change, you change with them. Listen to the trees blow and listen to what it's telling you and then re-strategize and keep things open. Stop taking yourself so seriously."

-Jacob Bacaner: Entrepreneur,
Fitness Model & Coach

"Having a child is definitely an adjustment! She's the boss of our daily schedules now so I've shifted my hours to work around hers. Usually she's up in the evenings, so I try not to do the bulk of my work then anymore. Instead, I find myself waking up earlier and getting started then. Or finishing something late at nights when she's asleep. I also try to stay way more focused when I do sit down to write or work because I have a limited amount of time in which to get something done. In a way, it's focused me even more. I find myself booming with ideas now though. I look at her and ideas light up. I've been playing guitar to her and singing and just connecting with her on a very deep, musical, spiritual level. I can't even try to put this into words. I'm more sentimental now than I was before. I think about her listening to these songs 10, 15, 20 years from now. The work I do with Elfenworks seems to have shifted meaning too. There's a very personal stake in it for me now."
–Alex Bondarev: Refugee & Indie Singer-Songwriter from The Bronx

"You're always growing and it's always going to be the next thing. It's never going to feel completely fulfilling. That's when it becomes important to have those relationships around you to fulfill that need inside of you. Because work is great and achieving things is amazing but, I'm a workaholic, I was for such a long time. Just going, going, going. I let a lot of my friendships fall to the wayside. I didn't see my family for a while. It left me feeling very empty. It's not until I found that work life balance where I get more out of my accomplishments because I've got that other piece of the puzzle there." –Suzanne Paulinski: Mindset Coach for Musicians & Industry Professionals

"I have my support friends that I always call and they help me gain clarity. Just find who are your support people- people that nourish your creativity, they know who you are and will help you when things get foggy. They help you gain a different perspective or just shake you up a little bit."
-Arta Cakaj, MS, LCAT: Wholehearted Art Therapy

"The love and balance of my family (husband and children), my art, my spirituality and freedom in the comfort of being me are most rewarding. I also love spending quality time by myself. It helps me clear my thoughts and hear my own voice."
-Alyscia Cunningham: Entrepreneur,
Author, Filmmaker & Photographer

On a daily basis, find your individual rewards and make time to enjoy them. That might be creating a project that is just yours, volunteering for a good cause, taking a class or spending time with your family. Most important to remember is that we are human beings and deserve to enjoy life's rewards. Do not punish yourself to detention in a job you hate just to make money, and then get caught up in the cycle of needing more money, wanting more money, and never having enough. Money is temporary. It is an illusion of status that we use to measure other people. Why not measure each other by the value we bring to each other's life? Why do we just accept this irrelevant collection of paper status that generations have agreed on as a way to categorize and oppress others?

"You have to let go- that's the biggest lesson of minimal- ism. What you surround yourself with is what's of value to you in your life. Everything else just takes up your energy because it's drawing your attention to it. What you want to focus that energy on is your creative endeavors, is the life

that you want to lead, the vision. I'm living it right now I think this is what's been helping me be successful as a minimalist, as a creative person, feeling connected to the flow of creative sources in my life and I think it's all related."
-Magdalena Reilly: Documentary Filmmaker, Podcast Host, Minimalist & World Traveler

"How do we create that joy, that is the challenge? How do we make the changes because what are the effects of staying unhappy at our job- it will make us sick. So it is good to think what are the steps that will make me happy? What are the fun things that I like to do that maybe I can do outside the job? Or in the job? We have to rethink how we see the boss or reinterpret the job. It's like a mental shifting of gears and when we find ourselves staying in that 'this job is horrendous. I want to get out.' It's a day by day thing. When you get home you don't have to see your boss. I can enjoy my family now and the next day is another time with family. It's a very strong lesson in stress management. It's a powerful lesson- how am I able to face a very difficult situation? This is the teacher. If I can face this, I can face any job. That is the challenge."
-Alma-Villegas Schwalbenberg, PHD

Happiness is something we can attain multiple times a day. Whereas being rich or famous is dependent on so many outside factors that we have no control over. If we are accepting other people's assessment of our value, we will always be comparing. The grass will always look greener on the other side. If we have a 9-to-5, we will pine for that freelance lifestyle where others are seemingly always on vacation, having a great life and making six figures. If we are freelance, we are comparing our inconsistent income and lack of benefits, to the stable and cushy benefits of a 9-to-5 job.

Life is short. Don't waste the time you have on this earth chasing what other people have. Figure out what makes YOU happy. Your answers will be unique to you.

> "I'm currently reading the story of philosophy by Will Durant and it hits Socrates, Plato, Aristotle, Francis Bacon, and Nietzsche, all these different influential philosophers. There's this one thing they all try to accomplish to answer the same question which is: 'what does it mean to live a good life? How is it best to live? Should we be focusing on the word happiness? Is that the end goal? Or is it fulfillment or excitement?' A lot of people want a job that makes them happy but I think a better word for that would be excitement. It's different for everyone."
> *-Alex Wood, co-founder of HoneLife*
> *and the Variety Seeker Tribe*

A job cannot make us happy. We can choose to be happy and make choices that help keep us there mentally. Ultimately though happiness is a choice no matter what situation we are in. I have noticed both as a freelancer and when I was working full time that my anxiety is a personal struggle. The biggest anxiety trigger for me is fear of the future. Thoughts about all the million possible ways that something can go wrong, or right. I start planning out ways to get to those multiple destinations, and then get disappointed when something doesn't pan out the way I had planned. Thinking about the present moment is what keeps me from anxiety and disappointment. For example if I am just starting to edit a documentary, thoughts will go through my mind, much like everyone else, of creating the BEST documentary in the whole world and making people cry, winning awards and becoming rich. Is it just me?

These expectations make it harder to focus on the tedious steps that are needed for the editing process. Similarly, when I don't have next month's freelance assignments lined up, or my calendar looks pretty empty going forward, I am filled with anxiety and fear of failure. I fill my anxiety hole of emptiness with searching for full time jobs and eating sweet things. This is not healthy, of course. Mindfulness is my way of combating anxiety because I can make a list of the things I need to do, effectively getting those things off my mind. It also keeps me focused on what I can control and allows me reflect on my past and current experiences. Reflection is so important and we often forget to do it because life is so fast-paced. This is what leads us to make the same wrong decisions again and again. I have to actively take the time needed to reflect, create a list whatever I want to do, write it down so it's out of my head, and then force myself to be in the moment focused on one thing at a time.

> *"We had a table reading at my office in Manhattan and the young actress said 'this is going to be so successful'. And I stopped her right there. This, the fact that we're all sitting here right now, this is the success. This table reading was the success. If you have to look forward to the next thing, how could you stop to enjoy what's happening right now?"*
> *-Elaine Del Valle: Film & TV*
> *Director, Producer & Actress*

Gratitude is my other weapon against anxiety, and it comes in handy most as a freelancer. At least once a day, I take time to realize and acknowledge the things I have in my life that are precious and special. Sometimes it is realizing that I have simple things like running water, a bed to sleep in, and food. We don't often think about the people who don't have what we take for granted, but many citizens of this planet do not have these luxuries.

On days when I'm feeling particularly down in the dumps, I have to channel my gratitude for the more extraordinary things that I have, which others do not. The people I love, and my health (which was not always this good). Mindfulness is the twin sister of gratitude for me. Not identical but there is not one without the other. Most of us tend to get caught up in thoughts of the past, present or future. The present thoughts are necessary to executing the task at hand, and staying grounded. When I can focus on the here and now, and have gratitude for all the great things in my life, I am choosing to be happy. You can do the same thing even if you aren't where you want to be yet. You can be proud of the efforts you've made thus far and glad that you have a strategy in place. This strategy or plan is a guide and it will change over time. Expect that you will have to modify the plan and go with the flow of life. The key is being positive and open to opportunities as they are presented to us. If we know ourselves well enough, we can use those opportunities to better ourselves which will take us where we want to go.

> *"Looking forward, mindfulness is a big thing. Mindful to the here and now, because it's here and now that creation starts- that you build your future. Just to face what's in front of you to enjoy it to trust your process. It's a different time table, but I always like the comparison of a seed to grow into a plant to bear fruit. What happens if you pluck the fruit unripe a mango or banana? That is the effect of rushing too. There is a process that we have to respect if it comes to fruition the way that we want it. Patience is a virtue and it's a lesson in patience but also a lesson in knowing the right time. I like that notion of waiting for it to ripen."*
> *-Alma-Villegas Schwalbenberg, PHD*

> *"When people have a clarity of mind, people are little bit nicer to each other, then people maybe are a little bit more under- standing, and maybe we can get along a little bit more, and*

the world isn't so bad because I know in today's times we have so much complexity in the political system, in our daily lives, our struggles, and the last thing we want is just more stuff on top of all these ideas and concepts. So [minimalism] it's a way for me to bring myself down to earth and just see things as they are, enjoy the moment, live for the day."
—Magdalena Reilly: Documentary Filmmaker, Podcast Host, Minimalist & World Traveler

There are a million experts out there who pretend to have the one correct answer when it comes to mindset practices. Truth is, it's different for everyone. We all have to find our own motivation to be happy, and stay that way. For me, I use gratitude and mindfulness to combat my anxiety and future-thinking tendencies. For the next person, that isn't a problem, and gratitude might not work. Whatever mindset techniques work for you, I suggest that you make it a habit of doing them daily. Don't be afraid to modify suggested exercises and techniques you may find in this book, and elsewhere. When you find something that works once, write it down. It's easy to forget these things and constantly be searching. That is life. We are forever in search of the ultimate happiness. Without reflection, we don't realize what is working for us. The negatives then start to have a louder voice, and they gang up on us until we are surrounded by negativity. Start leaving yourself reminders of what makes you happy in life. It will remind you of the incentives to stay that way.

Wishing you happiness in your career, your life and your mind.

*

ABOUT THE AUTHOR

Laura Meoli-Ferrigon is a seasoned content creator, podcast host & educator with 10 years of experience in Multimedia Production. Her achievements include a NY Emmy Award for her video producing/editing at CUNY, seven Telly Awards and multiple festival wins for her projects, "Give a Little," "Women of Action," "Perspective," and the "Granville T. Woods Documentary."

As founder of LoudaVision Productions, she helps her clients promote their business, products and services so they can build an online presence and reach a larger audience. LoudaVision Productions creates digital media including logos, graphics, video, audio and social media content. Her goal as a business owner is to deliver high-end results with a personal touch.

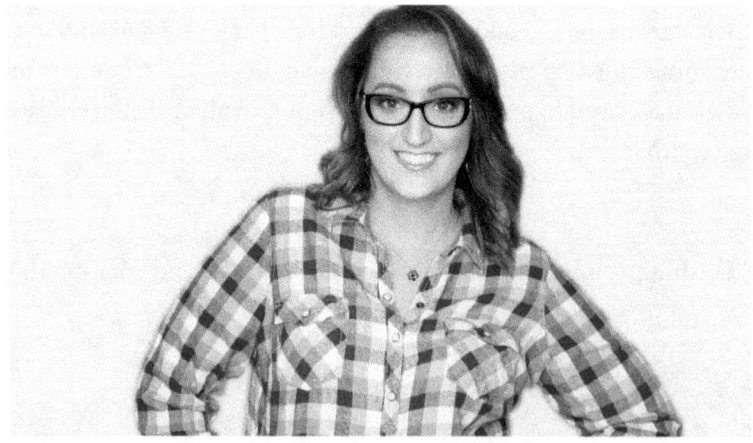

An educator at heart, Laura currently leads film production & podcasting classes for all ages, and conducts 1-on-1 private tutoring.

Laura hosts the LoudaVision Podcast to help creative people turn their passion into a career. The experience of producing this podcast inspired her to write the book you are currently reading. In the future, Laura hopes to travel the world and use her creativity to inspire others to be their best self.

For more information about the author, including samples of her work, please visit www.LauraMeoli.com and connect on social media @LoudaVision

www.ingramcontent.com/pod-product-compliance
Lightning Source LLC
Chambersburg PA
CBHW060827170526
45158CB00001B/107